PRAISE FOR
CHANGING THE GAME

"Intelligent, thoughtful, and complete. A must-read if you want to learn about interactive entertainment."

—Strauss Zelnick, founder of ZelnickMedia, Chairman of Take-Two Interactive Software, Inc., and former President and CEO of BMG Entertainment

"*Changing the Game* describes how innovative communities form around games and how many firms in the game industry are learning to work effectively with innovating users of their products. Companies in many industries will find these examples helpful, as we all move into the emerging new era of user-centered innovation."

—Prof. Eric Von Hippel, T. Wilson Professor of Management, MIT-Sloan School of Management

"David Edery and Ethan Mollick take on one of the most important issues of 21st-century entertainment and marketing—how the blending of video games with consumer marketing is deeply transforming both areas. This book is required reading for those interested in understanding both present opportunities and future growth in interactive entertainment."

—Jeff Bell, former Corporate Vice President of Global Marketing, Interactive Entertainment Business at Microsoft Corporation

Changing THE Game

Changing THE Game

How Video Games Are Transforming the Future of Business

David Edery and Ethan Mollick

Vice President, Publisher: Tim Moore
Associate Publisher and Director of Marketing: Amy Neidlinger
Acquisitions Editor: Martha Cooley
Editorial Assistant: Heather Luciano
Development Editor: Russ Hall
Operations Manager: Gina Kanouse
Digital Marketing Manager: Julie Phifer
Publicity Manager: Laura Czaja
Assistant Marketing Manager: Megan Colvin
Marketing Assistant: Brandon Smith
Cover Designer: Chuti Prasertsith
Managing Editor: Kristy Hart
Project Editor: Betsy Harris
Copy Editor: Cheri Clark
Proofreader: Heather Waye Arle
Indexer: Erika Millen
Senior Compositor: Gloria Schurick
Manufacturing Buyer: Dan Uhrig

© 2009 by Pearson Education, Inc.
Publishing as FT Press
Upper Saddle River, New Jersey 07458

FT Press offers excellent discounts on this book when ordered in quantity for bulk purchases or special sales. For more information, please contact U.S. Corporate and Government Sales, 1-800-382-3419, corpsales@pearsontechgroup.com. For sales outside the U.S., please contact International Sales at international@pearson.com.

This book was not sponsored or endorsed by Microsoft.

Printed in the United States of America
First Printing October 2008
ISBN-10: 0-13-235781-x
ISBN-13: 978-0-13-235781-4
Pearson Education LTD.
Pearson Education Australia PTY, Limited.
Pearson Education Singapore, Pte. Ltd.
Pearson Education North Asia, Ltd.
Pearson Education Canada, Ltd.
Pearson Educatión de Mexico, S.A. de C.V.
Pearson Education—Japan
Pearson Education Malaysia, Pte. Ltd.

Library of Congress Cataloging-in-Publication Data

Changing the game : how video games are transforming the future of business / David Edery, Ethan Mollick.
   p. cm.
  ISBN 0-13-235781-X (hbk. : alk. paper) 1. Video games industry. 2. Target marketing. I. Edery, David, 1976- II. Mollick, Ethan, 1975-
  HD9993.E452C39 2009
  658.4'0353—dc22
                                2008022302

CONTENTS

ACKNOWLEDGMENTS

This book could not have been written without the generosity and assistance of a great many people. This includes the dozens and dozens of people who agreed to be interviewed for the book, and to share their insights and knowledge with us. To all of you, we give our most sincere thanks. Of course, any errors, omissions, and controversial opinions expressed in this book are solely our responsibility.

Although it would be impossible to name everyone who contributed to this book, directly or indirectly, there are a few people in particular to whom we owe a special debt of gratitude, and whom we would like to acknowledge:

We would like to thank our friends at MIT for their invaluable guidance over the past several years. Dr. Henry Jenkins has been a mentor to David for the past several years, and his wisdom has helped shape much of our thinking about games. Many members of the business school faculties of MIT and Harvard have helped shape Ethan's approach to research (and this book) in innumerable ways, with profound thanks going to Professors Eric von Hippel, Karim Lakhani, Tom Malone, and Ezra Zuckerman, as well as many others. Additionally, some of the material in this book is connected with Ethan's academic research on the game industry, which is graciously funded in part by the Kauffman Foundation.

We would also like to thank David's colleagues at Microsoft, whose shared experience and wisdom spared us countless hours of work and made this book far better than it otherwise would have been. Bella Acharya, for her invaluable insights into the world of advertising and games. Ross Smith, for his boundless enthusiasm and willingness to share. Scott Austin, for his consistent support, encouragement, advice, and, most of all, friendship. And finally, a special thanks to Bryan Trussel, who saw the value in this project and opened the doors to it.

We are particularly thankful to our many friends who served as sounding boards for our not-always-fully-baked ideas, and whose feedback on early drafts of this book improved it tremendously. Professor Stacy Wood, for her invaluable help navigating the complex realm of consumer behavior research. Kim Pallister, for his sharp wit and excellent ideas. Daniel Cook, for his unmatched insight into the nature of games and play. Jeremy Tobacman, for his brilliance and generosity of spirit. John Miller, for his brutally honest (and helpful) advice. Soren Johnson, for his deep expertise and precision. Ben Gannon and Kelly McNeil, for their unwavering support and friendship. Bill Ferguson, for his profound thoughts on how we should think about games. Johanna Klein, for perhaps our most inspirational review. Jonathan Lewin, for the executive perspective. Barbara Barry, for her encyclopedic knowledge. Nick Maynard, for his focus on how games can help improve lives. The Greater New England Books and Bagels Society, for its collective literary expertise. And, most especially, thanks to Ilya Vedrashko, for his inspiring thoughts and—though he doesn't know it—for inadvertently setting the wheels in motion that led to the creation of this book in the first place!

Of course, we cannot possibly forget our families, whose love, encouragement, understanding, and advice underlies every single one of our accomplishments, not just this one. Thank you for everything, and especially for tolerating us while this book was being written. And thank you for reading innumerable drafts of our book and helping us move forward when we needed a shove. We promise to make up for the unwashed dishes, unreturned phone calls, unwalked dogs, and missed dinners. Somehow.

And last, but certainly not least, we would like to thank our editors, Russ Hall, Betsy Harris, and Martha Cooley, as well as the other people at Pearson who have played critical roles in getting this book into your hands. Martha, what can we possibly say to you, other than that we are truly in your debt. Thank you for believing in us and in this book!

About the Authors

David Edery is the Worldwide Games Portfolio Manager for Microsoft's Xbox Live Arcade. He is also a research affiliate of the MIT Comparative Media Studies Program. Prior to joining Microsoft, David was the MIT CMS Program's Associate Director for Special Projects. During that time, David cofounded the Convergence Culture Consortium, a research partnership with corporations such as MTV Networks and Turner Broadcasting. David also managed Cyclescore, a research project combining video games and exercise. David received his MBA from the MIT Sloan School of Management and his BA from Brandeis University. He has published articles in the *Harvard Business Review* and several game industry publications and has spoken at many entertainment industry conferences.

Ethan Mollick studies innovation and entrepreneurship in the game industry at the MIT Sloan School of Management. He holds an MBA from MIT and a BA from Harvard University. He has consulted for companies ranging from General Mills to Eli Lilly on issues related to innovation and strategy. He has also worked extensively on using games for teaching and training, including on the DARWARS project of the Defense Advanced Research Projects Agency. He was a founder of eMeta Corporation, the world's largest supplier of software for selling content online, which was sold to Macrovision in 2006. Prior to eMeta, he was a consultant for Mercer Management Consulting. He has published articles in scholarly journals, the *Sloan Management Review*, and *Wired* magazine, and has spoken at numerous conferences.

PART I

INTRODUCTION

Many of our friends like to tease us about our work and research. "Getting paid to play games," they say with a laugh, and it's hard not to smile when they do. There's no question that we love our work, and we don't mind the jabs. But what our friends don't realize, and what we hope to demonstrate through this book, is that work and games are not actually an unusual or antagonistic combination. In fact, companies of all shapes and sizes have begun to use games to revolutionize the way they interact with customers and employees, becoming more competitive and more profitable as a result.

From our vantage points in academia and within the game industry, we have watched as games have become a powerful tool through which organizations teach, persuade, and motivate people. Microsoft, for example, has used games to painlessly and cost-effectively *quadruple* voluntary employee participation in important (but tedious) tasks, like testing Windows Vista for bugs. Medical schools have used game-like simulators to train surgeons, reducing their error rate in practice by a factor of six. A recruiting game developed by the U.S. Army, for just 0.25% of the Army's total advertising budget, has had more impact on new recruits than all other forms of Army advertising combined. And Google is using video games to turn its visitors into a giant, voluntary labor force—encouraging them to manually label the millions of images found on the Web that Google's computers cannot identify on their own.

These are just a few of the examples that we introduce in *Changing the Game*, which begins with a discussion of how games and marketing have become a powerful combination, continues with an exploration of how games are being used to train and recruit employees, and ends with a look at the ways that games can be used to fundamentally change the way that companies do their day-to-day business. And although we've tried very hard to give specific, actionable advice that businesspeople can use to harness the power of games, we've also attempted to paint a broader picture of the dramatic impact that games are having on the world in general.

Games can make it fun for employees to learn how to manage a supply chain. Games can encourage customers to voluntarily spend hours learning about the features of a product. Games can encompass massive economies of virtual goods and services that are worth billions of real-world dollars. All of this—and much more—is happening right now at the intersection of business and games, and the forward-thinking companies at that junction have already begun to reap the great rewards of their effort. Games are transforming the nature of work and play in so many ways that, whether you work in a business, governmental organization, or non-profit, you can almost certainly find a way to take advantage of games to better accomplish your goals.

So, are you ready to play?

CHAPTER 1

AN INTRODUCTION TO GAMES, AND WHY THEY MATTER

These are good times for the video game industry. While growth in the movie industry has been slow and while the music business has contracted, games have grown at double-digit rates. Games are now on the verge of eclipsing the music industry[1] and have already surpassed Hollywood box office revenues.[2] Microsoft's *Halo 3*, one of the most anticipated video games ever launched, earned $170 million in the United States alone within 24 hours—more than the theatrical release of the movie *Spider-Man 3* or the novel *Harry Potter and the Deathly Hallows*.[3] And if you're not impressed by those numbers, consider this: A survey taken in 2007 found that more people in Calgary, Toronto, and Halifax could identify a photo of Nintendo's famous video game character, Mario, than could identify a photo of Canada's Prime Minister, Stephen Harper.[4] Not half bad for a fictional Italian plumber.

So, we'll take it for granted that you're probably somewhat familiar with video games. Nevertheless, even game industry analysts occasionally struggle to keep abreast of major happenings in the game space, which has evolved as rapidly as it has grown. In fact, we're willing to bet that the vast majority of people have no idea just how varied and far-reaching games have become. This chapter provides an overview of the current state of video games, and introduces a few concepts that will help you understand why games matter to the business world.

Why Games Matter

To some of us, everything in life looks like a game—especially business. There are the rules of the game (legal restrictions, generally accepted accounting principles). There are referees (trade bodies, courts). There are high scores (market capitalization) and there are levels of progression (director becomes VP becomes SVP, just as a level 20 wizard becomes a level 30 archmage, or a tennis player becomes a "pro"). There is cheating (fraud, corporate espionage) and there is teamwork (from internal cooperation to corporate alliances). The games we play when we are children, be they Little League baseball or cops and robbers, prepare us for the more serious games we play as adults.

Yet despite the preponderance of evidence that gameplay is a crucial communications medium and training ground for children, despite the prevalence of games in our society, and despite the meteoric rise of video games as a profoundly influential and profitable medium, the word "game" continues to have a negative connotation in the workplace. It is our contention that games, and most especially video games, not only belong in the workplace, but can make all the difference between success and failure. The key is to harness the properties of games that make them so uniquely compelling. Which invites the question "What are those properties, and why are games compelling?"

This is not a simple question to answer. One could argue that games are compelling because they entertain hundreds of millions of people all over the world, and there is certainly truth to that. But entertainment is just a symptom of gameplay, not the explanation of why it captures our attention and imagination. The answer to our question is ultimately much deeper and more interesting than that.

Games are compelling because, at their best, they represent the very essence of what drives people to think, to cooperate, and to create. Learning is not "work" in the context of a game—it is puzzle-solving, exploration, and experimentation. Cooperation is not a "necessary evil" in the context of a game—it is the best part of the experience. While many communities struggle to foster the most basic level of civic engagement, game-playing communities are remarkably active, engaged, and generous with their time and effort. How many companies can claim that a significant percentage of their customers voluntarily create and disseminate assets that dramatically increase the value of their products? As we will discuss in greater detail later in the book, a large number of video game companies can.

This book's purpose is to help you think about how video games are leading to the transformation of the wider business world, if not the world in general. Many of these changes, like using games for advertising and marketing purposes, have been under way for many years. Yet more transformative changes, like the use of games to spur innovation or harness collective intelligence, are still primarily being incubated in research labs and at universities. In this book's three major sections, "Games and Customers," "Games and Employees," and "Games and the Future of Business," we discuss how companies are using games to change how they interact with customers and potential customers, how they interact with employees and potential employees, and, finally, how companies are using games to change the way they inherently function, in general. Throughout the book, we try to keep the focus on what makes games special—interactivity, immersion, and fun—and what that means for businesses.

Before we dive deeper, we would like to stress one very important thing: Games must be played to be truly understood, or, at the very least, they must be carefully observed. A quick description of any game will be, at best, boring *("The goal of Tetris is to make little blocks fall into holes between other little blocks")* and, at worst, incomprehensible *("Dwarf Fortress can be won by digging lava traps while avoiding elephants and preventing your carpenters from becoming possessed*"—that latter one is a real game, by the way.) To make our descriptions more meaningful, we have put together a Web site, www.ChangingTheGameBook.com, which includes links to screenshots, videos, and playable versions of the games that we describe. Take a look and play a few of the games—it will make your reading experience much more meaningful. And, after all, it isn't often that you get to play games and call it work…though by the end of this book, we hope you'll agree that perhaps it *should* be!

Who Plays What on Which

For some people, their first experience with video games consisted of standing in front of an arcade machine, watching lines of incoming *Space Invaders* descend inexorably closer to the gun turret at the bottom of the screen. Or maybe it was sitting on a couch in front of the original Nintendo Entertainment System, challenging a friend to a relatively primitive game of electronic football. Others might claim that they have never played a video game of any kind, but the odds are that they have, at very least, played *Solitaire* or *Minesweeper* on a Windows computer—perhaps to pass the time during a boring conference call.

Despite being a relatively young industry, video games have a rich heritage. They were being built on the sly by bored mainframe computer programmers back in the 1950s, so that by the 1980s the basic elements of today's industry were already in place. Video games first became popular via arcade machines, represented by the iconic *Pac-Man* game sitting alongside pinball machines in a local pizza parlor or bar. But soon after arcade machines became an international phenomenon, two ways of playing games at home appeared: the dedicated console, such as the classic Atari 2600, and the personal computer. Through booms and busts, all three methods of playing games are still with us, though the arcade is a mere shadow of its former self.

The big winner over the past decade has been the dedicated gaming console, the latest incarnations of which are Microsoft's Xbox 360, Nintendo's Wii, and Sony's PlayStation 3, as well as their portable companions, the Nintendo DS and the Sony PSP. These specialized consoles have come to dominate the attention of the game industry, though PC games remain highly competitive, especially in certain genres. In addition, the cellular phone has recently become a widely prevalent and lucrative gaming platform, especially in regions of the world such as India, where phone ownership greatly exceeds computer and console ownership. And, of course, new gaming platforms seem to evolve almost daily—the personal video units on airplanes, the latest set-top boxes from cable companies, Apple's ubiquitous iPod…the list never stops growing.

Ultimately, these machines all serve as vehicles for delivering video game content itself. According to the MobyGames database (an online encyclopedia), there are at least 21,000 different games that have been commercially released in one form or another in the past 30 years, and that's just scratching the surface. Tens of thousands of additional games—many of them free to play—have been released online by various organizations and talented individuals. Most games, commercial or otherwise, fall into relatively well-established genres such as puzzle games, racing games, and strategy games. It would require an entire book just to describe these genres in significant detail, so, for the purpose of discussing games more generally, we would like to introduce two different dimensions along which most games can be categorized.

Casual and enthusiast games: Games that most people would consider "pick up and play," that do not demand great dexterity, and that can be played for short periods (but often are played for hours!) are called *casual* games. Many arcade games and most puzzle games, like *Pac-Man* and *Tetris*, respectively, fit into this category. Anyone can play a casual game for a few minutes and immediately understand the basic mechanics that make it fun. Casual games thrive on the Web and are common on portable devices like mobile phones. They are played by a remarkably large and broad audience: 52% are female,[5] and a substantial percentage of the total player population is over the age of 35. More than 150 million people worldwide play free casual games,[6] usually on their PCs or phones.

The opposite end of the spectrum are those games for the *enthusiast*, which tend to involve more intricate plotlines and complex gameplay, and may require tens of hours of playtime to complete. Enthusiast games are what many people think of when they imagine the stereotypical video game—the fast-paced shooting game played by a group of teenage boys; the complicated simulation replicating the Battle of Gettysburg; the incredibly realistic-looking virtual basketball game; and the latest *Pokémon* monster-training game being played by a group of children. Enthusiast games like these make up the majority of video games that are sold for home consoles like the Xbox 360 and PlayStation 3. They often have extremely large development budgets, ranging from $5 to $30 million, and the most high-profile of these games are launched with the same marketing theatrics as a Hollywood blockbuster.

Single-player and multiplayer games: To really understand the world of video games, however, we need to consider a second dimension of gameplay: sociability. Video games have progressed far beyond the stereotypical awkward, antisocial player sitting alone on a couch and have embraced the importance of companionship and community. Many of the most popular video games, both enthusiast and casual, feature compelling modes in which friends and/or strangers can play together.

This represents the second dimension in our diagram, which stretches from *single-player* to *multiplayer*. We start with games that are dedicated to solo play, progressing to those that support a couple of people playing together, to those that support teams of dozens of players in contest with one another, and, finally, to so-called massively multiplayer online games (MMOGs), in which hundreds or thousands of players participate in the same game world at the same time.

To demonstrate how games fit on our diagram, we have selected five relatively famous and interesting games that nicely illustrate the fundamental attributes of their genre, as shown in Figure 1.1.

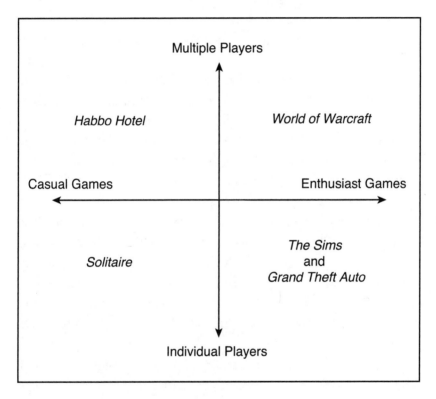

Figure 1.1 Placing five popular games according to which dimensions they fall in.

Single-Player, Enthusiast: *Grand Theft Auto 3*

Because the single-player enthusiast category of games is incredibly diverse, it's worth illustrating it with two very different examples of best-selling games. The first is *Grand Theft Auto 3*, also known as

GTA3. It was released in 2001 and remains one of the best-selling, highest-rated, and most controversial video games of all time. *GTA3* helped define an entirely new genre now known as the "sandbox game."

These games, like a sandbox full of toys, encourage players to experiment with their environment, without being constrained to a specific plotline or course of action. In the case of *GTA3* and its sequels, the "sandbox" is an entire virtual city full of realistic-looking buildings, vehicles, and people. You can drive from industrial zones, to commercial districts, to suburban neighborhoods. When you walk past a hospital, you actually overhear its residents discussing medical issues. Businessmen will pass you on the sidewalk, bitterly complaining about how hard they work. *GTA3* is alive with virtual residents of all types and ages, all of whom are just going along with their daily business...until you fire a gun into the air, that is. Then everyone nearby runs for cover.[7]

GTA3 enables its players to indulge in criminal acts, such as stealing cars, killing people, and consorting with prostitutes. These activities are packaged into a complex story of betrayal and revenge, which is slowly revealed to players as they complete missions throughout the city. But ultimately, a player can just as easily choose to ignore the plot and the missions and have fun however they see fit.

The impressive level of detail in *GTA3* and its sequels does not end with realistic-looking buildings or animated pedestrians. Players can dress their character in new clothes, feed them at fast-food restaurants such as "Cluckin' Bells" (which, when done excessively, will make the character fat and slow), and even earn money for their character by delivering pizzas or driving a cab. There are approximately 50 different vehicles in the game, all of which can be hijacked and driven around the city. The vehicles themselves are highly distinctive—from ponderous flatbed trucks to speedy sports cars to ambulances (which, ironically, can be used to help injured people after you've hijacked them!). And if you get into an accident, parts of your car will actually fly off, making your once-attractive ride look more like a salvage operation.

Even details like the presence of in-car radios were not neglected by the developers of *GTA3*. As you drive around the city, you can tune in to no fewer than nine radio stations, each of which plays a different style of music, from classical music to hip-hop to reggae. Interestingly, despite all the effort put into *GTA3*'s driving experience, the game rewards players who *don't* choose to drive everywhere, by making their character more fit and more capable of running long distances. Subtle (and surprisingly thoughtful) touches like this are precisely the sort of thing that turned *GTA3* into a massive commercial success. Of course, *GTA3* receives more attention for its darker features—for example, the ability to run over pedestrians in a speeding car, perhaps after shooting them first. These aspects of *GTA3* have led at least one critic to brand it a "murder simulator," and, although that is an extremely overdramatic description at best, there is no doubt that *GTA3* is a very violent game.

When it was first released, *GTA3* stood out in part because it was so unique, in part because its vast virtual environments were so realistic, and in part because *GTA3* recognized that game players often *like* to test the limits of the games they play. A rich, well-designed game that clearly encourages exploration and experimentation was bound to be a smash hit. Today, there are many other games that have adopted *GTA*'s "sandbox" style of play, and many of those feature remarkably large, complex, and realistic environments. These virtual environments are, in many cases, ideal settings for in-game advertising and training simulations; the potential for both is discussed later in this book.

Single-Player, Enthusiast: *The Sims*

The Sims and its sequel, the not-so-originally-named *The Sims 2*, are the best-selling PC games of all time, and are in many ways the polar opposites of *GTA3*. Whereas *GTA3* commonly serves as a sandbox for mayhem, *The Sims* is more like a virtual dollhouse or interactive soap opera. Players of *The Sims* control a household full of simulated people, or "Sims," with very human needs such as career growth, companionship, hunger, and sleep. These Sims eat pizza and watch TV, play with one another and with visiting Sims, and leave home to attend school or go to work. Your job, as a player, is to keep them happy.

In a normal game, the level of personality expressed by virtual characters would not be sufficient to exclusively maintain a player's focus for extended periods—but *The Sims* is not a "normal" game. Sims have horoscopes and personality traits such as neatness and playfulness. They express a wide range of emotions, they age, and they pass their "genes" on to their virtual children. They even have memories; for example, a Sim will mourn the loss of a loved one long after that person has died. That's right—Sims pass away, too.

Figure 1.2 Sims indulging their creative side (*SimCity, The Sims,* and *The Sims 2* ™ and © of Electronic Arts Inc. Used with permission.)

While playing the game, players earn money that can be spent on virtual items for their Sims, such as furniture or home electronics. But even a brand-new flatscreen TV won't keep Sims happy for too long; there are always relationships to maintain, careers to advance, and more home furnishings to purchase. In the words of one author, "*The Sims* doesn't really feel like a game. It seems more like gardening, or fixing up your house. One of the game's small triumphs is to make work seem like fun."[8]

The Sims offers predefined characters and scenarios to play with; players are also invited to develop their own story lines and create their own Sims, which a great many players have done. On the official *The Sims* Web site, fans have submitted more than 125,000 stories about their Sims, many illustrated with movies taken within the game. *The Sims* shows what video games, at their best, can offer—an outlet for creativity, a new way to engage the world, and many hours of entertainment—all in one package.

As a result of its compelling gameplay and subject matter, *The Sims* has become not only the most popular computer game of all time, but also one of the most demographically diverse "enthusiast" games. It is played by more women than men (60% versus 40%) and by many adults in general. *The Sims* has also proven to be a remarkably fertile ground for real-world brands, through both the conscious efforts of advertisers and the spontaneous efforts of players. For example, players have reproduced and shared more than 1,400 car makes and models in *The Sims*, not to mention a fair percentage of the IKEA furniture catalog.

Together, *The Sims* and *GTA* show the wide-ranging appeal of enthusiast games, from the stereotypical male gamer to the stay-at-home mother. But enthusiast games, despite their large share of press attention, are ultimately just one portion of the video game world—which brings us to the booming market for casual games.

Single-Player, Casual: *Solitaire*

There are so many popular casual games that it was hard to choose one to showcase. But at day's end, there is one single-player, casual game that has entertained more people, and gained greater recognition, than possibly any other video game in history. That game, of course, is *Solitaire*. Since Microsoft included *Solitaire* with the Windows operating system, it has been accused of everything from rotting our brains to uncountable losses in corporate productivity. New York City Mayor Michael Bloomberg famously fired a member of his staff for openly playing the game,[9] while a North Carolina state senator once attempted to ban *Solitaire* from government-owned PCs.[10] It has been described as "easy to learn, hard to master," fun for a few minutes or a few hours, and a great way to de-stress after (or during) work. It is played by all major demographics: old and young, male and female, black and white. Not coincidentally, these are the ideal characteristics of any good casual game, of which *Solitaire* is but one example.

What you may not be aware of is that hundreds of video game versions of *Solitaire* exist today. Some are incorporated into Web sites—like MSN Games—as an advertising vehicle and traffic attractor. Some are made available free or via a paid download to your local PC. Some are built into specialized "game portals" like Pogo.com, a Web site that offers both free casual games and "premium" games that can be played only if you pay a subscription fee. Some can be purchased for use on devices as diverse as a cellphone or the Xbox 360. *Solitaire* has literally found its way to every corner of the world, on almost every modern consumer entertainment device. Although the various versions of *Solitaire* differ widely in terms of their graphical polish, their rule set, and even the existence of a plotline, at the end of the day they all trace their roots back to the original, simple, classic *Solitaire* card game.

Many other casual games, like *Bejeweled* and *Tetris*, have taken the world by storm since the first days of *Solitaire*. But until recently, these games were considered neither a major potential source of revenue by most video game companies, nor a useful media form by businesses. All of that has changed, and it is our contention that casual games like *Solitaire* represent an excellent platform for advertisers, as well as a useful model for any business seeking to understand how to distill engagement into its purest form.

Multiplayer, Enthusiast: *World of Warcraft*

Few games have more successfully captured the attention of consumers, investors, and academics than *World of Warcraft*, far and away the most famous of the wordily named "massively multiplayer online role-playing games" (MMORPG). *World of Warcraft* is, in the truest sense of the words, a "virtual world"—one that can support thousands of players simultaneously. Devotees of *World of Warcraft* create a character ("avatar") when first joining the game, then spend days, months, and even years joining forces with other players to explore continents, slay monsters, find rare items hidden throughout the world, and much more. It is extremely difficult to understand the scope of *World of Warcraft* without seeing it for yourself—players can literally spend hours running or flying nonstop across dramatically varied and richly populated terrain. In fact, many players of *World of Warcraft* claim to enjoy the game in large part because they simply enjoy "seeing the sights." Those sights include underground cities, murky swamps, troll-infested jungles, scorpion-filled deserts, and beautiful beaches—all of which seem even more remarkable when viewed from the back of a soaring gryphon.

Figure 1.3 A player of *World of Warcraft* riding a gryphon (*World of Warcraft*®
provided courtesy of Blizzard Entertainment, Inc.)

Players of *World of Warcraft* often band together in groups of 2 to 40 people in order to help one another travel through dangerous locations, kill enemies, and complete quests. But regardless of whether someone prefers to play *World of Warcraft* alone or in a group, they will experience the social aspects of the game. If they visit a city, they will walk past tens or hundreds of player avatars, all engaged in conversation with one another as well as other activities. If they purchase a virtual item from a store or from another player, their purchase affects the global economy and contributes to changes in price and supply. *World of Warcraft* is truly a massively multiplayer game—even for loners.

As of the time of this writing, *World of Warcraft* has more than 9 million subscribers. U.S. residents pay an impressive $15 per month for the privilege of playing the game, in addition to approximately $50 when first purchasing it. In 2007 alone, *World of Warcraft* generated $1.1 billion,[11] and there is currently no end in sight to its revenues. It has attracted players from all over the world, and has even been called "the new golf" by Silicon Valley entrepreneurs looking for a hip new environment in which to do their professional networking.[12]

World of Warcraft is remarkable for many reasons, not the least of which are the various ways in which it deeply engages its players. For example, over the course of several months, a typical player might spend many hours simply customizing the appearance of her avatar, for both aesthetic and strategic purposes. She might work for days to acquire a particularly powerful and impressive-looking sword, and after she has acquired that sword, she might spend several more days earning enough gold to buy an enchantment that makes the sword glow with flames. Through mechanisms like this, the developers of *World of Warcraft* have proven adept at channeling the seemingly inexhaustible energy of their players, a major challenge for a game that bills monthly and is played by many customers for several hours a day.

To help put this in context, imagine if someone asked you to perform the same menial task 50 times in a row; odds are you probably wouldn't appreciate it. But *World of Warcraft* and similar games ask this of players all the time by presenting them with "quests" that involve significant repetition, generally by requiring rote travel across significant distances, or by requiring the player to slay a given type of monster over and over again. The reward for these activities is generally the advancement of your avatar's strengths and abilities, a useful or attractive virtual item, and the opportunity to progress further down the game's storyline. The phenomenon of performing the same task in a game repeatedly is called "grinding," and it adequately describes one of the less stimulating aspects of *World of Warcraft* in specific, and many MMORPGs in general. In more extreme but not unusual cases, players may spend upwards of 50 hours literally slaying and reslaying the same monster, which reappears under certain conditions, in hopes of attaining a very rare item that is awarded with low probability upon the death of that monster. These players are effectively *paying for the privilege of grinding* because of the compelling incentives and activities woven around it. How many companies, even with the incentive of a paycheck, fail to encourage the reliable execution of rote tasks? But perhaps the more interesting question is this: Could games help businesses with this problem? We explore the answer to that question in Chapters 8 through 10.

Lastly, while we have mentioned the importance of virtual items and currency in this and other games, we have not yet touched on their "real-world value." As it turns out, many regular users of massively multiplayer games are willing to spend real money on virtual goods, even if such transactions are officially banned by the game's operator (as is the case with *World of Warcraft*). These transactions are common and lucrative enough that estimates of their total yearly value range from the hundreds of millions to the *billions* of dollars per year.

Games like *World of Warcraft* hint at potentially tremendous opportunities for businesses that are willing to explore exciting if unconventional strategies. We will explore these strategies, among others, in the "Games and the Future of Business" section at the end of this book.

Multiplayer, Casual: *Habbo Hotel*

Habbo Hotel is one of the most successful instances of a new breed of game that has taken the entertainment industry by storm. Although the ordinary person is much more likely to have heard of *World of Warcraft*, they are not more likely to have played it. *Habbo Hotel* has more than 97 million registered users, and attracts 9.5 million unique visitors a month,[13] only slightly less than *World of Warcraft*'s subscriber base and growing more quickly. It is targeted primarily at teens and has gained popularity all over the world, including the U.S. The user experience in *Habbo Hotel* is simple to enjoy but difficult to describe; in essence, everything takes place in a gigantic virtual hotel containing millions of rooms, each offering a different experience. Many of the rooms are "owned" by the players themselves; each user has a private space that they can decorate with virtual furniture and in which they can socialize with friends. But many other rooms are operated by *Habbo Hotel* itself or its advertising partners, and these rooms feature simple games, opportunities to win prizes, and more. They also often contain branded items and large virtual billboards that, when clicked, lead you to an advertiser's Web site.

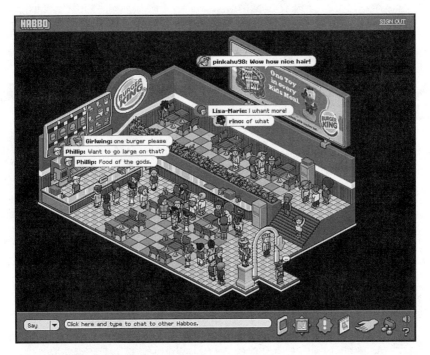

Figure 1.4 A Burger King–branded room in Habbo (Reprinted with the permission of Sulake Corporation)

Like *Solitaire*, our other "casual" case study, *Habbo Hotel* appeals to both males and females (51% and 49%, respectively), is easy to use, and is thematically inoffensive to just about anyone.

Like *World of Warcraft*, our massively multiplayer case study, *Habbo Hotel* brings many players together in a single virtual space, features customizable avatars and virtual currency, and encompasses a large number of different digital environments just waiting to be explored by curious players. *Habbo Hotel* has been described by its creators as a "gameless game,"[14] a place where people play together and are motivated in part by some of the traditional features of games (the opportunity to win "special" virtual items, for example), but where no unifying story or gameplay mechanic ties everything together. *Habbo Hotel* is as much a social network as it is a game, but people are clearly "playing" when they enter this virtual space. Role-playing, in particular, is a common activity. Players have been known to, for example, decorate a room as a police station, dress up like police, and pretend to monitor *Habbo Hotel*. Others have voluntarily re-created a McDonald's restaurant within the confines of their room and role-played serving hamburgers to lines of virtually hungry fellow avatars.[15] Of course, if players are doing this sort of thing voluntarily and without assistance, one wonders how McDonald's might be able to capitalize on the situation! User-generated content of this and many other kinds is ultimately at the heart of *Habbo Hotel*, and fostering it has proven key to the success of the game.

Habbo Hotel, like *World of Warcraft*, is difficult to truly comprehend without playing it for yourself. But unlike *World of Warcraft*, the barrier to entry is extremely low, which in part explains why *Habbo* has 86 million registered users. Sign up is free and takes seconds to complete. We highly encourage readers who are not familiar with *Habbo Hotel* or games like it to sign up and give it a spin. However, be prepared to not understand much of what the other players are saying—unless you're a teenager, that is.

Games and Virtual Worlds

The common thread tying together *World of Warcraft* and *Habbo Hotel* is that both take place in virtual worlds. After years of false starts—some readers may remember the "virtual reality" goggles and gloves of the early 1990s—virtual worlds are finally becoming a reality, thanks in large part to video games. These virtual worlds are almost exactly what they sound like—environments in which many players can interact with both each other and the environment, rather than spaces that necessarily attempt to ape reality.

Together, *Habbo Hotel* and *World of Warcraft* illustrate how different virtual worlds can be. *World of Warcraft* is a graphically impressive world full of beautiful scenery, in addition to a large population of elves, walking skeletons, and demons. *Habbo Hotel*, on the other hand, tends less toward graphical realism and more toward a stylized environment resembling a 1980s-era video game. Other virtual worlds might abandon the laws of physics, or skip human-looking characters in favor of talking animals and other make-believe creatures.

Regardless of their nature, virtual worlds are becoming increasingly popular, especially among the young. Recent trends suggest that by 2011, 54% of all U.S. teens and children will be using virtual worlds.[16] The trend is even more impressive in countries like China, where Internet-connected youths are nearly five times more likely than Americans to claim they lead a "parallel life" online.[17]

Although there are many interesting virtual worlds, a significant amount of corporate and academic effort is being poured into one world in particular: *Second Life*. Though not the largest virtual world by a long shot, with just under 600,000 unique visitors a month at the end of 2007, *Second Life* has managed to achieve a unique position in the minds of businesspeople and academics through a combination of clever features and terrific hype.

Launched in 2003 by Linden Labs, *Second Life* can barely be called a game, though it makes heavy use of video game technologies. In truth, *Second Life* is more of a giant virtual sandbox; it lacks an overarching plotline or theme, and unlike other games and virtual worlds we will discuss, effectively 100% of the content in *Second Life* is created by its users. These users can customize everything from the laws of physics to the color of the sky within the virtual territory they control—another significant point of differentiation between *Second Life* and other virtual worlds. *Second Life* also has a relatively unique business model; it generates much of its revenue through the sale and recurring taxation of virtual territory.

Figure 1.5 One of the more realistic-looking locales in Second Life
(© 2008, Linden Research, Inc. All Rights Reserved.)

A few key attributes have contributed to the early success of *Second Life*. First, it is free to basic users. This means that there is a large pool of potential *Second Life* visitors—as many as eight million, though many do not return after their initial visit. Second, Linden Labs has provided a set of relatively simple tools that enable users to create their own content, ranging from T-shirts to skyscrapers to elaborate games, and has allowed users to retain the copyright on these creations. This has resulted in a flourishing online economy, priced in the local currency of Linden Dollars, which players use to buy and sell virtual items, buildings, and territory, among other things. Linden Dollars float against other currencies, allowing users to exchange real and virtual money freely, and enabling a small percentage of *Second Life* players to earn comfortable livings off their virtual work.

Finally, Linden Labs has embraced the corporate and academic worlds, encouraging a wide range of organizations to experiment in *Second Life*. Among these experiments are virtual ethics counseling sessions for British Petroleum employees,[18] product co-creation labs by Alcatel-Lucent,[19] no fewer than three official national embassies, campaign rallies for national political candidates, and a very large number of advertising efforts by companies ranging from Dell to Adidas. These advertising efforts, in particular, have come under increasing scrutiny as of late. Critics have called advertising within *Second Life* both expensive and ineffective, and companies focused on enabling advertising in *Second Life* have recently experienced financial difficulties.[20] We explore these criticisms in more detail in Chapter 4, "Adverworlds, *Second Life*, and Blurred Reality."

The verdict is still out on *Second Life* as a whole, but the popularity of *Second Life*, *World of Warcraft*, *Habbo Hotel*, and other virtual worlds in general is guaranteed to persist. Research company Virtual Worlds Management, for example, reports that over $1 billion was invested in virtual worlds from October 2006 to October 2007,[21] though a more conservative estimate would still be a staggering $500 million. As virtual worlds become increasingly popular, profitable, and easy to leverage by corporations seeking ways to entertain and connect with customers and employees, we expect their tremendous growth to continue.

Games and User-Created Content

One of the most important business lessons to be drawn from video games started, as such things rarely do, with Smurfs and Nazis. In 1983, one of the more popular PC games was an arcade-style game called *Castle Wolfenstein*. The object of the game was to sneak through a Nazi castle in order to retrieve secret war plans. Soon after the game was released, two suburban high-school kids managed to modify the game so that, instead of fighting Nazis, the player was fighting Smurfs, and the frightening shouts of the Nazis became the jaunty and ever-recognizable Smurf theme. It wasn't much, but *Castle Smurfenstein* represented the first well-known, user-created "mod" (short for modification) of a computer game.

In the quarter century since, mods and other content usually created for free by consumers have become critical factors in the success of video games. Consider *Half-Life*, an enthusiast game in which the player must escape an alien invasion. *Half-Life* was released in 1998, but a decade later almost 100,000 people a week are still playing a modified version of *Half-Life* called *Counter-Strike*. That's just one mod out of more than 570 created and made available by players of *Half-Life*.[22] All of these mods require the original game to play, which has driven sales of the original, decade-old game to more than 11 million units—an astonishing number in the enthusiast video game market.

What game companies have discovered is how to tap into the tremendous energy of user communities. To understand how potentially powerful these communities can be, look no further than the community surrounding *The Sims*. One major *Sims* user Web site, among several others, has more than 670,000 active members who have created more than 358,000 pieces of content for the game.[23] Those numbers are astonishing in their own right, considering the amount of free value derived by EA, the maker of *The Sims*. And this is not amateur or easy work. A survey of Sims modders found that over half of all active modders spent more than six hours a week developing new content for free, and over 12% spent more than 20 hours a week.[24] Another economic study found that video game users also reduced costs for game companies by helping each other solve technical problems, to the extent that they solved 1,300% more problems than the paid support staff of the companies behind the games.[25] The power of video games to inspire communities is unquestionably one of their most compelling features. We discuss how businesses are leveraging this phenomenon throughout the book.

Games and Controversy

No introduction to the world of video games would be complete without an analysis of the controversy that occasionally surrounds them. Although games are frequently the subject of public scrutiny and debate, they are in reality not much different from other forms of media. (It seems ridiculous today, but the *Hardy Boys* books were once prominently described as equivalent to underage drinking, and likely to "blow out the brains" of the innocent boys who read them![26]) Critics, no doubt conscious of previously failed attempts to censor books, radio, television, and film, have attempted to differentiate their arguments against games by focusing on the interactive nature of the game-playing experience. Criticism typically focuses on one of two hot-button areas: violence and childhood obesity.

Violence: Games have been criticized as "excessively violent" for decades. Such criticism first reached fever pitch in 1992, when a popular game called *Mortal Kombat* enabled players to gruesomely slay an opponent by, for example, ripping off his head and holding it in the air while the spine dangled below. At the time of its release, *Mortal Kombat* was considered visually stunning, but its graphics pale in comparison to those of modern games. As the graphical fidelity of video games has improved, various social, professional, and governmental organizations have expressed increasing concern over the potential impact of "realistic" interactive violence on children. These fears have been intensified by reports from organizations such as the American Psychological Association, which have claimed to link violent games to increased aggression inside and outside the laboratory.[27]

These criticisms have been rebutted by various prominent independent academics and organizations. Most notably, the American Sociological Association (ASA) and British Board of Film Classification (BBFC) recently issued reports supportive of the video game industry. The ASA noted that in the ten years following the release of games such as *Doom* and *Mortal Kombat*, homicide arrest rates among juveniles fell by 77%,[28] an especially notable figure given that video game usage skyrocketed during the same time frame.

The ASA also found that much of the research employed against video games had decontextualized violence. In the words of the report, "Poverty, neighborhood instability, unemployment, and even family violence fall by the wayside in most of these studies. Ironically, even mental illness tends to be overlooked in this psychologically oriented research. Young people are seen as passive media consumers, uniquely and uniformly vulnerable to media messages." Likewise, after performing its own extensive research study, the BBFC found that "far from having a potentially negative impact on the reaction of the player, the very fact that they have to interact with the game seems to keep them more firmly rooted in reality. People who do not play games raise concerns about their engrossing nature, assuming that players are also emotionally engrossed. This research suggests the opposite; a range of factors seems to make them less emotionally involving than film or television."[29] This conclusion—that video games might actually exert *less* influence on aggression than film or television—is especially remarkable in light of the importance and charter of the organization that produced it.

Critics of the game industry frequently leap to the conclusion that video games are the cause of any tragedy, such as the Columbine school massacre, that involves young men and violence. However, the fact is that the *vast majority* of U.S. males age 14 to 34 have played video games. If the mere act of playing a game is to be considered statistically significant proof of a causal relationship, then games can be linked to just about anything—including acne, adolescent flirting, and the rising cost of gasoline. We are more persuaded by evidence that the Columbine shooters had been subject to consistent bullying than by the underwhelming coincidence that they—like everyone else their age—had played games.

Our convictions on this subject are backed by a recent study performed by the U.S. Secret Service, which examined each of the 37 non-gang and non-drug-related "targeted" U.S. school shootings and stabbings that took place from 1974 through 2000, including infamous incidents such as the Columbine massacre. The Secret Service found that there is no "profile" of a school shooter. In fact, only 1 in 8 of the perpetrators studied by the Secret Service showed any interest in violent video games, and only 1 in 4 liked violent movies.[30]

Lastly, an often-ignored but key argument against critics of violence in games is simply that games have a prominent rating system, much like movies do. That rating system can be used by parents to filter the games they are comfortable exposing their children to—an acceptable solution given that 90% of games are purchased by adults over the age of 18.[31]

Apathy and childhood obesity: Video games have been accused of contributing to the obesity epidemic in the United States. These accusations have not generally amounted to significant pressure on the industry, because games are not clearly at greater fault than television watching or Internet use. And although some studies have claimed to demonstrate a link between game playing and obesity, the same studies have noted that turning off the TV or the video game console would not ultimately solve the problem.[32]

Ironically, parents and governments alike have recently begun turning to video games in search of a solution to the obesity epidemic. Take the case of *Dance Dance Revolution (DDR)*, a game that is played by stepping on an electronic dance mat in tune with various high-energy dance tunes. At more advanced levels, it is literally impossible to play *DDR* without sweating profusely. The game has proven so successful at motivating people to physically engage (and, as a result, burn calories) that schools all across the United States are now installing *DDR* arcade machines on their premises. In fact, more than 1,500 schools are expected to install *DDR* by the end of the decade. West Virginia alone has committed to installing *DDR* in all 765 of its public schools by the end of 2008.[33] Similarly, the Nintendo Wii, a video game console recently released in the United States, looks poised to potentially become a weapon against the obesity epidemic, as gamers fervently swing its motion-sensitive controller while playing virtual games of tennis, boxing, and more. Ten years ago, the ordinary person would likely have associated video games with obesity; ten years from today, games will most likely be an important component in the exercise regimen of children everywhere.

It is important to recognize that the controversies surrounding video games exist, and that critics of games can be extremely passionate and political. However, as we have explained, games are no more harmful to people of all ages than film or television. The game industry is large and mature, and has long since adopted a rating system that is no less reliable than that employed by films the world over. And game technology, which can be used in so many interesting ways, is no more inherently "dangerous" than the Internet—commonly criticized, but ultimately vital to society as we know it today. In short, businesses can and should take advantage of games, as long as they approach them with the same level of care and awareness that they would apply to other mass-market media.

Games and the Future of Business

That games have been the focus of so much scrutiny is a reminder of how ubiquitous they have become. But despite the fact that games are played at home, during commutes, and practically everywhere else by hundreds of millions of people, they remain an untapped resource for many companies. By contrast, those businesses that have seen games as more than just a diversion, and fun as more than leisure, have started to reap the great rewards of their insight.

This book is a rejection of the notion that "all work" must necessarily mean "no play." It is a picture of a changing corporate landscape; of a growing gaming revolution that will touch every aspect of our work lives, from how we sell products, to how we are hired, to how we do our daily jobs.

Endnotes

1. Jacqui Cheng, "Report: Video Game Spending to Surpass Music Spending This Year," *Ars Technica* (2007), http://arstechnica.com/news.ars/post/20070623-report-video-game-spending-to-surpass-music-spending-this-year.html.

2. James Brightman, "Video Games Explode: Global Revenues Now on Par with Box Office," *GameDaily* (April 03, 2008), http://www.gamedaily.com/articles/news/video-games-explode-global-revenues-now-on-par-with-box-office/?biz=1.

3. "It's official:' Halo 3' Registers Biggest Day in US Entertainment History," *Major Nelson* (September 26, 2007), http://majornelson.com/archive/2007/09/26/it-s-official-quot-halo-3-quot-registers-biggest-day-in-us-entertainment-history.aspx.

4. Nintendo of Canada, "Italian Plumber More Recognizable than Harper, Dion," *Nintendo of Canada Press Release* (November 17, 2007), www.newswire.ca/en/releases/mmnr/Super_Mario_Galaxy/index.html.

5. Casual Games Association, "Casual Games Market Report 2007," (2007), http://www.casualconnect.org/newscontent/11-2007/CasualGamesMarketReport2007_Summary.pdf.

6. Beth A. Dillon "Event Wrap-Up: Casuality Seattle," *Gamasutra* (July 6, 2006), http://gamasutra.com/features/20060706/dillon_01.shtml.

7. IGN Staff, "Grand Theft Auto III Review," *IGN* (May 27, 2002), http://pc.ign.com/articles/360/360877p1.html.

8. John Seabrook, "Game Master," *The New Yorker* (2006).

9. Margaret Kane, "A Costly Game of Solitaire," *CNET News.com* (February 13, 2006), www.news.com/8301-10784_3-6038534-7.html.

10. Patrik Jonsson, "Is that a Spreadsheet on Your Screen or Solitaire," *Christian Science Monitor* (March 18, 2005), www.csmonitor.com/2005/0318/p01s02-ussc.html?s=t5.

11. Reena Jana and Matt Vella, "Activision-Vivendi's Game Changing Deal," *Businessweek* (December 4, 2007), www.businessweek.com/technology/content/dec2007/tc2007123_075300_page_2.htm.

12. Jane Pinckard, "Is World of Warcraft the New Golf?" *1UP* (February 8, 2006), 1up.com/do/newsStory?cId=3147826.

13. Sulake, "Quick Habbo Facts," (May, 2008), http://www.sulake.com/habbo/.

14. Brandon Sheffield, "Designing a Gameless Game" *Gamasutra* (October 10, 2007), www.gamasutra.com/view/feature/1946/designing_a_gameless_game_sulka_.php.

15. Christian Nutt, "Haro On Making Habbo A Success," *Gamasutra* (September 9, 2007), www.gamasutra.com/php-bin/news_index.php?story=15397.

16. Debra Aho Williamson, "Kids and Teens: Virtual Worlds Open a New Universe," *eMarketer* (September 2007), http://www.emarketer.com/Report.aspx?code=emarketer_2000437&tab=Toc&src=report_toc_reportsell.

17. IAC, "China Leads the US in Digital Self-Expression" Press Release (November 23, 2007), www.iac.com/index/news/press/IAC/press_release_detail.htm?id=8833.

18. Colleen Monahan, Kevin Harvey, and Lars Ullberg, "BP Tries *Second Life* for Employee Ethics Compliance," in *Second Life* Education Workshop Proceedings (2007).

19. "Alcatel-Lucent Launches Presence on *Second Life*(R) Virtual Reality Site to Explore the Potential Uses of Next-Generation Technologies, Including 4G Mobile Broadband Networks," Press Release (Oct 23, 2007).

20. Mary Jane Irwin, "Electric Sheep Lays Off 22 Second Life Developers," *Valleywag* (December 18, 2007), http://valleywag.com/tech/layoffs/electric-sheep-lays-off-22-second-life-developers-335353.php.

21. Virtual Worlds Management "$1 Billion Invested in 35 Virtual Worlds Companies from October 2006 to October 2007," Press release (2007), http://virtualworldsmanagement.com/2007/index.html.

22. "Half-Life," *ModDB*, Accessed May 2008, www.moddb.com/games/1/half-life/addons. Zeh Fernando, *Online Gaming Zeitgeist*, Accessed May 2008, www.onlinegamingzeitgeist.com/mods/.

23. Delphy, "Ads, MTS2 Stats, 2008, Servers, Donation Drive and Featuring a Hippo in a Bukkit!" *Mod The Sims* 2 (January 8, 2008), www.modthesims2.com/showthread.php?threadid=267348.

24. Reinhard Prügl, Martin Schreier, "Learning from Leading-Edge Customers at *The Sims*: Opening up the Innovation Process Using Toolkits," *R&D Management* 36.3 (2006) , 237–250.

25. L.B Jeppesen, "User Toolkits for Innovation: Consumers Support Each Other," *Journal of Product Innovation Management* 22.4 (2005), 347.

26. Marilyn Greenwald, "The Newspaper Reporter as Fiction Writer: The Tale of Franklin W. Dixon," Proceedings of the Annual Meeting of the Association for Education in Journalism and Mass Communication (86th, Kansas City, Missouri, July 30-August 2, 2003), History Division.

27. American Psychological Association, "Violent Video Games Can Increase Agression," Press Release (April 23, 2000), www.apa.org/releases/videogames.html.

28. Karen Sternheimer, "Do Video Games Kill?" *Contexts*, 6.1: 13-17, www.asanet.org/galleries/default-file/Winter07ContextsFeature.pdf.

29. British Board of Film Classification, "Playing Video Games—BBFC Publishes Research" (April 17, 2007), www.bbfc.co.uk/news/stories/20070417.html.

30. Lawrence Kutner and Cheryl K. Olson, "Myths About Violent Video Games and Children," *Grand Theft Childhood Web Site*. Accessed May 2008, www.grandtheftchildhood.com/GTC/Myths.html. Readers who are very interested in this subject may wish to pick up a copy of *Grand Theft Childhood*.

31. Entertainment Software Industry of Canada, "Facts & Research: Games & Violence," *ESA Canada Web Site*, www.theesa.ca/facts-gameviolence.html.

32. Aaron Levin, "Video Games, Not TV, Linked to Obesity in Kids," *Health Behavior News Service*, (March 17, 2004), www.cfah.org/hbns/news/video03-17-04.cfm.

33. Seth Schiesel, "PE Classes Turn to Video Games that Work Legs," *New York Time*, (April 30, 2007), www.nytimes.com/2007/04/30/health/30exer.html.

PART II

GAMES AND CUSTOMERS

On December 31, 2006, Burger King announced a whopping (pun intended) 40% increase in quarterly profit.[1] This increase was driven not by a popular new snack or clever TV advertisement, but by three Xbox games sold exclusively in Burger King restaurants across the United States for $3.99 each. Consumers flocked to Burger King, snapping up 3.2 million games in just a few months. And they didn't simply buy the games—they purchased meals that might otherwise have been consumed at competing fast-food chains across the street. Then consumers took the games home, where they played them for many hours. Each play session exposed consumers to the Burger King brand and its highly recognizable characters, such as the (slightly creepy) King himself and the Subservient Chicken. In other words, the games were not merely a one-time promotion like so many others in the fast-food industry; they were a Trojan horse into the home and a long-term advantage over mighty competitors like McDonald's.

Burger King is a great example of how firms can use games to transform their advertising strategy, but the use of games can go much further. Take the case of Ganz, a toy company that began distributing stuffed animals known as Webkinz in 2005. These cute but generic toys are no different from the many other playthings cluttering the shelves of children's stores across the nation, with one crucial exception. Each Webkinz toy comes with a multicharacter code that, when entered into the Webkinz.com Web site, results in the "adoption" of the pet you just purchased. In essence, Webkinz.com brings your toy to life online. The Webkinz.com world is filled with the virtual pets of other children, a wide variety of online games, and many opportunities to win virtual prizes, among other features. It converts a physical toy, which might merit a few minutes of attention a day, into hours of fun each week. (For reference, Webkinz visitors spend, on average, significantly more time on the site than Facebook or MySpace users spend on those sites.)[2] In just two years, more than one million Webkinz stuffed animals were sold, and in 2007 the Toy Industry Association named Webkinz the Specialty Toy of the Year.[3] For a mature industry like the toy business, Webkinz represents a revolutionary new direction. Other companies, including industry-stalwart Mattel, have since rushed to emulate the Webkinz phenomenon.

These are just two examples of ways in which games have recently become important tools for mature, mainstream industries. The next three chapters introduce a wide variety of game-based techniques that are being used by businesses to connect with customers. Chapter 2, "Advertising 'In' and 'Around' Games," explains how familiar advertising approaches like commercials and product placements have been integrated into video games. Chapter 3, "Advergames," discusses the rise of advergames, or games that have been created for the sole purpose of promoting a brand, like those developed by Burger King. Finally, Chapter 4, "Adverworlds, *Second Life*, and Blurred Reality," explores how companies have begun to harness the power of virtual worlds, and how advertisers are now blurring the lines between reality and games in their endless quest to engage audiences. Together, these techniques have injected more fun into the realm of marketing, and have transformed the way in which businesses relate to customers.

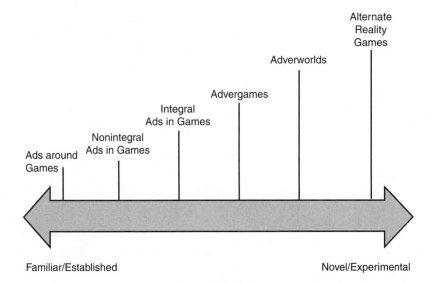

Figure 1 The various methods of using games to connect with customers, ranging from well-established methods that are now common in the gaming world, to more novel methods that have surfaced only in recent years.

Endnotes

1. James Orry, "Burger King Profits Up 40% Thanks to Video Games" *Videogamer.com* (January 1, 2007), http://www.videogamer.com/news/31-01-2007-4641.html.

2. Eugenia Levenson, "New 'Kinz on the Block" *Fortune Magazine* (February 16, 2007),http://money.cnn.com/magazines/fortune/fortune_archive/2007/03/05/8401272/index.htm.

3. Jacob Ogles, "How to Take Money from Kids: Sell Toys Both Physical and Virtual" *Wired Magazine* (July, 2007), http://www.wired.com/gadgets/miscellaneous/news/2007/07/webkinz.

CHAPTER 2

ADVERTISING "IN" AND "AROUND" GAMES

The 30-second television spot may be under siege by digital video recorders and changing media consumption habits, but the ten-second video advertisement is alive and well in the realm of video games. As are, for that matter, sponsorships, product placements, and other well-understood forms of advertising. Games are becoming as viable an advertising medium as television ever was—it just took a while for marketers to come around.

In fact, the simplest forms of game-based marketing are direct descendants of common advertising techniques, such as commercials and product placements, which were initially developed for print media, television, and film. These techniques are backed by decades of experience and research, so it's no surprise that marketers are applying them to games. But unlike television and film, games are an interactive medium, so they open up fascinating opportunities for new twists to old marketing methods.

Advertisements "Around" Games

"Advertisements around games" are advertisements experienced outside the context of actual gameplay. They're the equivalent of commercial breaks in a television show, corporate sponsorships of a theatrical performance, or ads appearing alongside a news article in a Web site. The most common examples of "advertisements around games" are banner ads that appear above a game in a Web browser and video ads that play before a game begins.

The opportunities to advertise around games have been driven primarily by the rise of the free video game market, which has grown exponentially in recent years. In addition to a large number of free online games that are released every month and supported with banner or video advertisements, older big-budget enthusiast games are now being re-released as free, ad-supported games as well. Consumers, accustomed to paying $50 or $60 for retail enthusiast games, have proven understandably receptive to these ad-supported versions.

Collectively, these games appeal to almost every demographic, which means if you're looking for a relatively easy way to reach a specific audience, ads around free games are a good option. For example, Web sites like Pogo.com feature a collection of casual games that attract millions of adult women, whereas an ad-supported, downloadable version of the enthusiast game *Prince of Persia: Sands of Time* appeals primarily to younger men.

Oftentimes, ads around games are no more interesting than ads around other types of online media, but there are indications that they may be more effective. For example, click-through rates for banner advertisements on major Web destinations such as Yahoo! and AOL have declined from an already underwhelming 0.75% to a near-rounding error of 0.27% in 2006, according to online advertising firm Eyeblaster[1]. Compare this to the effectiveness of video ads that were shown between gameplay sessions on Gamehouse.com, a video game portal operated by Real Networks. In 2007, Real reported a 10% click-through rate for these video ads,[2] a rate far higher than that of the ordinary Web banner. At least for the time being, consumers seem willing to reward advertisers with increased attention in exchange for free gameplay.

Furthermore, despite the familiar nature of advertising around games, some real innovation has taken place in this space. One example involves the virtual economies of online games like *Habbo Hotel*. The developers of these games often sell virtual currency to players in exchange for very real cash; players then use that currency to acquire in-game items like clothing, furniture, or weapons. In fact, when the developers of popular online games choose *not* to sell their virtual currency (requiring instead that players "earn it" through online activity), black markets tend to spring up. *World of Warcraft* serves as a particularly remarkable example of this. Many affluent *World of Warcraft* players, eager to acquire more virtual gold than they are physically able to earn by playing the game, have turned to unsanctioned third parties for satisfaction. These third-party brokers are fueled, in part, by tens and perhaps hundreds of thousands of Chinese laborers who earn a living by playing *World of Warcraft* and selling virtual gold.[3] The *New York Times* has reported that these laborers earn approximately 30¢ an hour, while the brokers they work through pocket millions of dollars—a significant chunk of the estimated $1.8 billion worldwide trade in virtual items.[4]

Savvy marketers have recognized virtual currency for what it is: a prime opportunity to generate goodwill by gifting game players with something that is deeply meaningful to them, but costs very little to produce. Take the case of *AdventureQuest*, an online game with 6.5 million players a month. More than 90 advertisers have signed up to sponsor the game's currency. Players of *AdventureQuest* are faced with an intriguing choice: Use real cash to buy virtual gold, or embrace a sponsor and receive gold free. Contrast this with other sponsorship opportunities—for example, a theatrical event with a ticket price of $50, sponsored by multiple different corporations, several of which are highlighted by the event host. How much value does the buyer of that $50 ticket really understand or believe that they are receiving from the sponsor? But the person who benefits from an *AdventureQuest* sponsorship can have no doubt as to its value—after all, the sponsorship just paid for a shiny new (albeit virtual) sword!

Advertisements around games may not always be sexy, but they are often easy to implement, easy to scale, and easy to target.

Companies looking for a simple way to dip their toes into the world of video games may want to consider these opportunities. There are, however, more interesting ways to use games as marketing vehicles—specifically, by advertising *within* games. Such advertisements, commonly called "product placements," are potentially much more powerful than typical film or television product placements. The trick, as always, is to leverage what makes games special—their interactivity.

Advertisements "In" Games

In a key moment in *Tom Clancy's Splinter Cell: Pandora Tomorrow,* government operative Sam Fisher crouches in the ductwork along the top of a bank vault while terrorists outside prepare to blast open the doors. At the bottom of the vault is a wounded security guard, the only surviving person who has seen the face of the terrorist mastermind behind the attack. As the bomb ticks away, the player quickly maneuvers Sam Fisher into the vault, and the action pauses as the dying guard hands Fisher a vital clue to the identity of his foe. The evidence appears in the form of a Sony Ericsson T637 mobile phone, whose bright screen displays a photo of the mastermind, which had been taken by the brave guard using the handset's built-in camera. The player knows that the fate of the world rests on that phone and the picture stored within it.

Tom Clancy's Splinter Cell: Pandora Tomorrow includes not only the aforementioned Sony Ericsson T637 phone, but also an advanced P900 mobile phone that is used by the player to read important mission data off a memory stick. By using the phones to progress through the game, players become highly familiar with them. And because the phones are tightly and sensibly integrated into the plot of the game, it is unlikely that they will be recognized by players as paid advertisements. This is just one example of the unique ways that marketers can leverage advertisements *in* games.

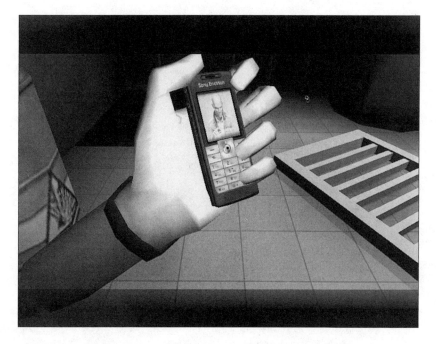

Figure 2.1 Sony Ericsson mobile phone in *Tom Clancy's Splinter Cell*
(Reprinted with the permission of Ubisoft Entertainment)

Product placements within media are by no means novel. They have appeared in films since the 1940s and have become increasingly common since then.[5] Sears is reported to have paid over $1 million to have its brand and products featured in ABC's *Extreme Makeover* reality television series, and Steven Spielberg's film blockbuster *Minority Report* was subsidized with $25 million in product placement deals made with Nokia, The Gap, and Lexus.[6]

Video games are no exception. The majority of modern sports and racing games are loaded with consumer brands, and other genres of games are quickly becoming popular with advertisers as well. Run around a virtual city, throw a football in a virtual stadium, or drive around a virtual racetrack, and odds are you will see an advertisement on a virtual billboard, recognizable retail stores like Pizza Hut, and vehicles embedded by Ford and Chrysler. When implemented correctly, these in-game advertisements can even improve the gameplay experience by making a virtual environment seem more realistic. After all, given the prevalence of brands in everyday life, it would be unnatural *not* to encounter them within games that purport to simulate reality. (Can you imagine visiting a sports stadium during a major event and not seeing a single ad?) In-game advertisements are also especially attractive in light of the fact that many games are played for tens or even hundreds of hours. No single television show or film can match that level of exposure.

Of course, an advertisement that looks natural on the hood of a NASCAR vehicle would look ridiculous on the side of a unicorn. But blending real-world brands with fantastical game environments is a surprisingly common mistake. For example, in 2007, Best Buy and 7-Eleven stores were integrated into a massively multiplayer game called *MapleStory*. Ironically, as of the time of this writing, the first sentence of the *MapleStory* information page reads: "You can explore a totally new and unknown world you have never been to." According to Nexon, *MapleStory*'s developer, 7-Eleven and Best Buy were even integrated into "appropriately themed quests" in the game.[7] Kill a dragon, get a Slurpee—nothing could seem more natural! Or, as one popular gaming Web site stated, "This is not cutting-edge. This is cutting-stupid."[8] Suffice it to say, this is a good example of how not to do a product placement within a game.

The best in-game advertisements are consistent with the spirit of a game in every way. For example, all the objects within a game, including embedded advertisements, must obey the same laws of physics, no matter how realistic or distorted those laws may be. In a NASCAR game meant to simulate real-life racing conditions, an advertiser's car cannot emerge from a crash completely unscathed. In an urban shooting game, billboards cannot prove immune to bullet holes even as the environment around them is pockmarked by a player's gunfire.

The negative impact of mismatched in-game advertising can be severe. Consumers, as well as the gaming press, have loudly denounced the most blatant offenders for shattering an otherwise immersive gameplay experience. And years of consumer psychology research across television, film, and games have shown that ill-fitting product placements lack effectiveness and can even result in negative brand attitudes. (Conversely, research has shown that well-executed product placements can be particularly influential.[9]) Given these issues, marketers should be careful not to forget what makes a product placement special—its ability to be perceived as a natural part of a game, *not* a paid advertisement.

Fortunately for advertisers, there are a reasonable number of games that are set in modern, realistic environments and are suitable for product placement. In 2005, 12 of the 20 best-selling PC titles were conceptually suitable, and 14 of the top 20 console titles were as well.[10] All told, approximately 40% of all retail video games can support in-game advertising.[11]

There are two types of in-game advertisements: those highly integrated into the gameplay experience, and those more peripheral to a game's action and plot. Peripheral advertisements are the most common form of in-game advertisements, mainly because it's easy to paste a brand onto the front of a virtual billboard or the side of a truck. Highly integrated product placements, such as the Sony Ericsson phones in *Splinter Cell*, are less common but extremely interesting from an advertising perspective.

Highly Integrated Product Placements

Highly integrated product placements are not new, nor are they unique to video games. Some of the most successful advertising campaigns in history have hinged on well-executed, highly integrated product placements. For example, if you've seen the movie *E. T.*, you're no doubt familiar with the candies used to lure that famous alien from his hiding place. Ironically, Mars passed on the opportunity to include M&Ms in *E.T.* out of fear the candy's brand could be harmed, thus handing Hershey a golden opportunity to revitalize Reese's Pieces, boosting sales by at least 65% and raising the candy out of relative obscurity.[12] Similarly, when BMW integrated its Z3 Roadster in the James Bond film *Goldeneye*, consumer and press enthusiasm proved absolutely tremendous; over $100 million worth of audience exposure was generated by that placement and the promotions associated with it.[13]

Much like the Sony Ericsson phones in *Splinter Cell*, both Reese's Pieces and the Z3 were tightly woven into the plots of *E.T.* and *Goldeneye*, respectively. But unlike film-based product placements, game-based placements have the additional advantage of interactivity. Consumers who play *Splinter Cell* become intimately familiar with some of the phones' key features—an effect that could have been further amplified if Sony Ericsson had chosen to integrate the phones into more missions, or had enabled the player to use them in more ways. (Ironically, you never actually use a Sony Ericsson phone to call someone during the game!) In other words, game-based product placements can not only demonstrate value, but also give players the opportunity to experience that value firsthand.[14]

Marketers have taken advantage of highly integrated video game advertisements to differing extents. Some have focused merely on story integration, whereas others have gone further. Players of *CSI: 3 Dimensions of Murder* store vital data on a virtual SanDisk Cruzer flash drive.[15] Players of *The Sims Online*, a massively multiplayer version of *The Sims*, were able to visit McDonald's kiosks to quell their Sim's hunger and increase their Sim's happiness level[16]—an interesting illustration of how games can "educate" consumers about a brand and its core attributes. Similarly, in the city-building game *SimCity Societies*, wind farms built by players to power their towns are branded by global energy giant BP, part of a move by the company to convey its "green" side to environmentally aware consumers. Players of *SimCity Societies* can also construct coal and nuclear plants, but because those power sources do not reinforce the message that BP is trying to deliver, they are conspicuously unbranded in the game.

Unfortunately, the very attributes that make highly integrated product placements an attractive advertising option also make them relatively challenging to implement. Because they require a significant amount of effort to integrate into gameplay, highly integrated product placements are more expensive than other forms of advertising in and around games. For similar reasons, these placements cannot be integrated into a game during its final stages of development. This means that advertisers may be forced to sign a highly integrated product placement deal over a year before the release of a game.

An Easier Way to Do Highly Integrated Product Placements

Although the best highly integrated product placements are almost always going to be the result of a thoughtful, highly coordinated effort planned well in advance of a game's release, there is another, perhaps easier, way to take advantage of this marketing strategy. Thanks to rising Internet usage, it has become common for game developers to offer "downloadable content" that expands the scope of previously released games. Consumers are often eager to embrace this content, which enables them to get more mileage out of their investment in a title. Having recognized the possibilities, Ford recently paid Electronic Arts to make a Ford Mustang downloadable car available to players of *The Sims*. More than one million players voluntarily downloaded the Mustang so that their Sims would finally have a cool car to drive. This improved the game, made EA customers happy, and no doubt made the marketing executives at Ford very happy!

Peripheral Product Placements

Not all product placements must be highly integrated into the gameplay or story. Advertisements that are less central to the action, such as a Coca-Cola billboard or vending machine on the side of a road, are examples of "peripheral" product placements. Think of these advertisements as part of the landscape—seen, but not explicitly brought to the players' attention.

Peripheral product placements can come in many forms. Some are two-dimensional, such as road signs, or the sides of a box. Some are three-dimensional objects, such as a can of soda or a 747 flying overhead. The clothing worn by characters in a game can be branded. Character dialogue can be tweaked to contain subtle brand references. In a rich enough game, there are thousands of ways to potentially embed a peripheral product placement.

Games can also support "dynamic advertisements," which are peripheral product placements that can be embedded into (and removed from) a video game *after* it has already entered the market, as long as the game is connected to the Internet. Dynamic advertising technology is most commonly used to insert peripheral placements onto simple, two-dimensional spaces, such as billboards, the sides of a truck, or the front of a vending machine.

Dynamic advertisements have a number of interesting advantages over other forms of advertising in games. Because they can be inserted into a game after its development is completed, advertisers can take advantage of them without many months of advance planning. Dynamic ads also have the potential to make a game feel even more realistic than static ads. Cory Van Arsdale, General Manager of Microsoft's Massive dynamic advertising network, explains: "Imagine you're in a first-person shooter game and you're in Times Square hunting terrorists. What would Times Square be like with no ads? If you insert generic ads, you've made it look a little more like Times Square. And with dynamic ads, when you play the game, you might see a trailer for a movie that is currently playing in theaters, as opposed to a trailer three months old. That's what Times Square should feel like."

The Psychology of Product Placements

Whereas highly integrated product placements increase the likelihood that people will consciously remember a brand, peripheral product placements operate on a more subconscious level. Psychologists have linked this phenomenon to two related concepts, "mere exposure" and "priming," which together help explain why even when we don't consciously notice a peripheral product placement, it can nevertheless stick in our memory in a way that increases our preference for a brand.[17] Most advertisements, not just game-based advertisements, depend heavily on these psychological effects to achieve their desired result. However, peripheral product placements within games are especially well-suited to take advantage of these effects, mainly because gameplay is such an involving activity.[18] The higher our level of involvement with a medium, the more effective a product placement can be.

Our current understanding of the mere exposure effect and of priming is rooted in a set of fascinating studies that have been performed over the past few decades. In one experiment, people who spoke no Japanese were exposed to pictures of unfamiliar Japanese characters. Later, they were shown the same Japanese characters and asked which ones they preferred the most. The more someone had been exposed to a given character, the more likely they were to indicate preference for it.[19] This study has been replicated in many ways; in one interesting case, people were exposed to images of irregular shapes for such brief periods of time that the images were effectively imperceptible. Nevertheless, when later asked to select from among different shapes, people were inevitably more attracted to those they had seen for mere milliseconds earlier on.[20]

Studies of priming have demonstrated that exposure to words, images, and ideas can influence our purchase behavior. This effect has been observed inside and outside the laboratory, both intentionally and unintentionally. For example, when NASA's Mars Pathfinder successfully landed in 1997, Mars candy bar sales unexpectedly spiked![21] All of this has great relevance to video games, many of which offer numerous opportunities for subtle, quick, and repeated exposures to product placements in a highly involving environment.

Interestingly, gameplay-induced moods have a significant effect on the way that peripheral product placements are perceived and internalized. For example, studies have shown that happy film and television segments are likely to increase the effectiveness of associated advertisements, while sad or upsetting segments may have the opposite effect.[22] For example, focus group respondents who viewed *The Silence of the Lambs* reported a negative association between Arby's restaurants and the killer, Buffalo Bill, because of a scene showing discarded Arby's wrappers and cups in the killer's home.[23] There is little reason to believe that the positive and negative spillover effects demonstrated in TV and film won't also be present in video games.

Details aside, both peripheral and highly integrated product placements are becoming increasingly important ways for advertisers to get their message across. The choice among them depends primarily on timing and budgetary considerations, as well as whether an advertiser needs to communicate a simple or complex message to consumers. Figure 2.2 illustrates how an advertiser might decide which kind of product placement to use.

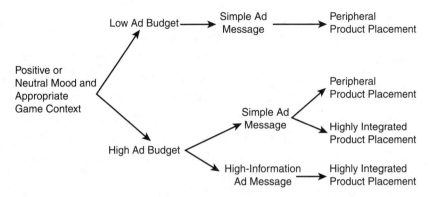

Figure 2.2 The decision process for choosing between peripheral and highly integrated product placements.

Placements in Virtual Worlds

Many virtual worlds are suitable environments for product placements. Each of these worlds has its own culture, just like any real-world city with thousands of residents. So advertisers need to make sure that their advertisements respect that culture and add value to the world. Sometimes "adding value" is simply making an environment seem more realistic, and in that regard, advertisements such as billboards may work well for virtual worlds with modern, realistic themes. However, there are more creative ways for advertisers to do placements in virtual worlds. World Wrestling Entertainment (WWE) has provided us with an interesting and amusing example.

To promote its SummerSlam pay-per-view event, the WWE virtually introduced one of its wrestlers, John Cena, to the players of *Gaia Online* (a free virtual world somewhat like *Habbo Hotel*). Cena's avatar was introduced by the founders of *Gaia Online*, whose own avatars are extremely well-known to the *Gaia* community. Cena (or someone representing him) spent the next few days interacting with the community and sharing information about the

WWE's upcoming SummerSlam event. On the third day of the promotion, a mysterious new user named "RKO" joined *Gaia Online* and began threatening to beat up John Cena as well as the founders of *Gaia*. Residents of *Gaia* were enabled to choose sides; those who joined RKO received a virtual folding chair—a classic weapon in the WWE universe—while those who supported Cena and the founders received other items. On the final day of the promotion, RKO was revealed to be Randy Orton, a WWE wrestler and the chief "bad guy" of SummerSlam.

The *Gaia* WWE promotion is a fine example of fundamentally harnessing virtual worlds for marketing purposes. The WWE created an activity that people could enjoy, and did so in a virtual world already partially populated by WWE fans—guaranteeing a base level of enthusiasm for the promotion that appears to have proven infectious. According to Joe Hyrkin, Vice President of Business Development for *Gaia Online*, the WWE promotion ultimately attracted the attention of more than 200,000 *Gaia* users and helped boost SummerSlam's ratings.

Sulake Corporation, the developer of *Habbo Hotel*, has recently begun experimenting with a more hands-off approach to product placements. Like many other virtual worlds, *Habbo Hotel* is characterized, in part, by the great enthusiasm of its players for rare and attractive virtual items, which players use to decorate their online rooms and avatars. Sulake has cleverly leveraged this enthusiasm by occasionally releasing rare sponsored objects into the *Habbo Hotel* universe. These include items like virtual props from Paramount's 2008 film *The Spiderwick Chronicles*. The items are not necessarily part of a massive promotion—they are simply interesting objects that, by virtue of their rarity, become much-desired among users of *Habbo Hotel*.

Habbo Hotel's Lead Concept Designer, Sulka Haro, explains it this way: "The level of commitment that we've seen to high-quality, sponsored virtual objects is way higher than the commitment to cheap, mass-produced giveaways, like the key chains or cheap pens you might find distributed at a conference. Everyone in *Habbo Hotel* knows about the existence of rare items and wants to have some of their own. So, our sponsors are associating themselves with something very valuable in the minds of our users." And, of course, the rarity of an item increases the likelihood that users will want to display it proudly, which increases the likelihood that other users will see it.

The Two Keys to Success When Advertising in Games

Among the keys to success when advertising in games are the following:

Invest the appropriate amount of effort: Implementing an advertisement within a game—even a peripheral, dynamic advertisement—takes time and forethought if you want to do it right. At the very least, you must ensure that your brand fits within the context of the game, and that your brand is presented in a way that enhances the player's experience. To achieve a truly effective advertisement, you must go beyond basic fit and actively seek the in-game moments that are most conducive to advertising. (In other words, while it may be possible to realistically place your brand at the scene of a horrifying nuclear catastrophe, you generally shouldn't.)

Don't be afraid to have a little fun: Companies can use the interactive elements of gameplay to make advertisements not only more memorable, but even more fun (or funny!). Imagine the following scenario: A player of *The Sims* feeds one of her household Sims too often, which causes the Sim to become fat, which then causes the Sim's girlfriend or boyfriend to break up with the Sim. The depressed Sim might then turn on a television for comfort, which, ironically, would be playing an advertisement for Jenny Craig diet products. Or imagine if, whenever you demolished a car in *Grand Theft Auto*, there was a small chance that a bus would drive by with the following advertisement painted on it: "GEICO auto insurance: You wish you had it!"

Endnotes

1. Catherine Holahan and Robert D. Hof, "So Many Ads, So Few Clicks" *BusinessWeek* (November 8, 2007), www.businessweek.com/magazine/content/07_46/b4058053.htm.

2. Yuanzhe (Michael) Cai, *Electronic Gaming in the Digital Home: Game Advertising* (Parks Associates, 2007).

3. Ge Jin, *The Real Price Of Virtual Gold*, (documentary film available at MTV Networks) (2006), www.mtv.com/overdrive/?id=1545907&vid=120059.

4. Julian Dibbell, "The Life of the Chinese Gold Farmer," *The New York Times* (June 17, 2007), www.nytimes.com/2007/06/17/magazine/17lootfarmers-t.html?pagewanted=1&_r=1.

5. Michelle R. Nelson, "Recall of Brand Placements in Computer/Video Games," *Journal of Advertising Research* (University of Wisconsin-Madison, April 2002).

6. Lars-Peter Schneider and T. Bettina Cornwell, "Cashing In On Crashes Via Brand Placement in Computer Games," *International Journal of Advertising*, 24(3) (2005): 321–343.

7. David Radd, "Nexon Retail Partners Integrated into MapleStory," *GameDaily* (December 4, 2007), www.gamedaily.com/articles/news/nexon-retail-partners-integrated-into-maplestory/18741/.

8. Mike Fahey, "7-Eleven to Appear in MapleStory, Vice Versa," *Kotaku* (November 29, 2007), http://kotaku.com/gaming/stupid-marketing-tricks/7+eleven-to-appear-in-maplestory-vice-versa-328068.php.

9. L. J. Shrum, ed., *The Psychology of Entertainment Media: Blurring the Lines Between Entertainment and Persuasion* (Lawrence Erlbaum: 2003).

10. Ilya Vedrashko, "Advertising in Computer Games" (2006), http://gamesbrandsplay.com/files/vedrashko_advertising_in_games.pdf.

11. See note 2.

12. Barbara Mikkelson, "Taking it E.T.," *Snopes Urban Legends Reference Page* (2007), www.snopes.com/business/market/mandms.asp.

13. Siva K. Balasubramanian, James A. Karrh, and Hemant Patwardhan, "Audience Response to Product Placements: An Integrative Framework and Future Research Agenda," *Journal of Advertising* (2006).

14. This unique property of games has been studied extensively by Dr. Ian Bogost, the author of *Persuasive Games*, who argues that highly integrated product placements can be used to make persuasive arguments of many kinds, including arguments about brand value, stylishness, and function.

15. See note 10.

16. Ian Bogost, *Persuasive Games: The Expressive Power of Videogames* (MIT Press: 2007).

17. See note 13.

18. Dan M. Grigorovici and Corina D. Constantin, "Experiencing Interactive Advertising beyond Rich Media: Impacts of Ad Type and Presence on Brand Effectiveness in 3D Gaming Immersive Virtual Environments," *Journal of Interactive Advertising* (2004).

19. R. L. Moreland and R. B. Zajonc, "Is Stimulus Recognition a Necessary Condition for the Occurrence of Exposure Effects?" *Journal of Personality and Social Psychology* (1977).

20. W. R. Kunst-Wilson and R. B. Zajonc, "Affective Discrimination of Stimuli That Cannot Be Recognized," *Science* (1980).

21. Larry Yu, "What You See Affects What You Get," *MIT Sloan Management Review* (Summer 2007).

22. See note 13.

23. John A. McCarty, "Product Placement: The Nature of the Practice and Potential Avenues of Inquiry," in *The Psychology of Entertainment Media: Blurring the Lines Between Entertainment and Persuasion*, edited, by L.J. Shrum (Lawrence Erlbaum: 2003).

CHAPTER 3

ADVERGAMES

If a product placement within a game sounds like it could be effective, how about a game designed for the sole purpose of advertising a brand or product? "Advergames" are video games that are funded directly by an advertiser and are often distributed free of charge to consumers. Like highly integrated product placements, well-designed advergames have the power to entertain consumers in an engaging and even informative way. Unlike product placements, advergames offer businesses more control over the context in which their brand is experienced by consumers, and saves them the possible hassle of operating within the constraints imposed by game developers.

Although some advergames have cost several million dollars to develop, many are produced for anywhere between $25,000 and $750,000. One example is *Jeep 4x4: Trail Of Life*, which cost DaimlerChrysler well under a million dollars. It was released in 2001 to promote the Wrangler Rubicon, a $32,000 off-road vehicle. *Jeep 4x4* enabled consumers to virtually experience driving the "extra-rugged" Rubicon through an exotic Mayan jungle. Although the game was never intended to compete on equal terms with commercially released driving games, it was nevertheless downloaded by more than 380,000 consumers,[1] many of whom provided their names and e-mail addresses in the process. Ultimately, 14% of the first orders for the Rubicon came from people who had registered for the game, and 25,000 Rubicons were sold in the first year—over

300% more than Chrysler initially expected. The company was so impressed that it subsequently increased its advergaming budget at the expense of its TV budget.

Automobiles and Gaming Ingenuity

It would be easy to dismiss the auto industry as blessed with an easy product to market via games, but companies like Chrysler have not simply churned out driving simulations. For example, to promote the "Stow and Go" foldaway seating system in its minivans, Chrysler developed an advergame that challenges players to cram as many packages as possible into a Stow and Go–equipped vehicle. The packages are acquired from real stores such as Bed Bath & Beyond, which makes this an interesting early example of cross-promotional advertising in games.

Stow 'n Go Challenge was a simple puzzle game— inexpensive to develop and reasonably appealing to the consumer demographic that Chrysler was targeting with its minivans. The game attracted 100,000 consumers, all of whom voluntarily opted in to play the game and share their contact information with Chrysler.

Auto manufacturers are not the only advertisers embracing advergames. This rapidly growing category has attracted a wide range of companies that, in 2006, used advergames to reach more than 21 million people in the U.S. alone. Increasing corporate interest is expected to boost advergame spending from $110 million in 2006 to $532 million in 2012.[2] Companies are developing advergames for large consumer audiences and for small but lucrative niche audiences all over the world. Take as an example Intel's recently launched, massively multiplayer advergame, *Silicon*

Commander. The game, which pits fleets of Intel-powered robots against one another, was marketed exclusively to IT managers in Asia, and offered prizes such as Apple iPods and Dell notebooks. *Silicon Commander* attracted 12,000 highly engaged players—a great number, given the size of the target audience—and ultimately exceeded Intel's expectations, as we'll explore in more detail later in this chapter.

Some advertisers, having recognized the great potential of advergames, have begun to position themselves as regular suppliers of video game content to their customers, putting themselves in direct competition with professional video game publishers and dedicated gaming Web sites. Wrigley's Candystand.com, a Web site launched in 1997 to promote Wrigley candies, is one prominent example. Since launch, Candystand has grown to comprise a huge selection of free branded games, becoming a major entertainment destination in the process. Although the cost of maintaining Candystand is no doubt significant, the site attracts more than four million unique visitors each month, which translates into tremendous exposure for the various Wrigley brands featured within. Impressively, in early 2007 Wrigley even launched a special version of Candystand.com for the Nintendo Wii, putting it ahead of many dedicated game publishers and developers in capitalizing on the Web-browsing capabilities of that popular console.[3]

Independent research on the effectiveness of advergames is rare, but encouraging to advertisers. One recent academic study, designed to measure the impact of advergames on children, evaluated *Froot Loops Toss*—a casual game developed by Kellogg and hosted on the Froot Loops Web site until 2005.[4] In the game, players could score ten points by tossing Fruit Loops into a monster's mouth, or five points by tossing real fruit into the monster's mouth. Given the major ethical questions about the appropriateness of advertising to children, the authors of this study sought to determine what impact, if any, *Froot Loops Toss* would have on children's brand preference, and on their belief that Froot Loops are more or less healthy than real fruit. In the end, the study determined that *Froot Loops Toss* had no impact on children's perceptions of the cereal's relative healthiness. The study did find, however, that preference for Fruit Loops over other popular cereals nearly doubled in test groups of children age seven and eight. These results suggest that although companies should always take great care to obey ethical standards when advertising to children (and perhaps Kellogg nearly, if unintentionally, crossed a line here), they should also not be afraid to leverage the tremendous potential of advergames.

Demonstrating a Brand's Values with Advergames

Most advergames won't win any prizes for creativity. Stereotypical examples are a checkers game with the pieces replaced by M&Ms candies, or a pool table with the Jack Daniel's logo painted on its surface. These advergames, though uninventive, are inexpensive to develop, and serve the purpose of linking a brand to an appealing lifestyle or activity. The more interesting advergames are those that can be called "demonstrative" or "persuasive" because they actively communicate a meaningful message to consumers.[5]

Chrysler's *Jeep 4x4* is a persuasive advergame. It demonstrates the value of a Wrangler Rubicon by enabling players to virtually drive the vehicle under challenging road conditions. The game takes place in a dense jungle, where players must drive off-road, up steep inclines, and through running water to achieve their objectives. In some ways, this experience is more convincing than a real-life test drive; after all, how many auto dealerships will let you handle a vehicle under dangerous road conditions? Jeff Bell, formerly the Vice President of Chrysler's Jeep division and now Corporate Vice President of Global Marketing for Microsoft's Interactive Entertainment Business, confirmed that realistically conveying the

Rubicon's handling and performance was a key goal of the game. "We were very, very disciplined about the physics. If you rolled over the Jeep, the Jeep was rolled over and you had to start again. You couldn't crawl up surfaces that a real-world Jeep actually couldn't crawl up. We even gave the developer our CAD/CAM drawings, technical specifications, and test results so they wouldn't have to make anything up. It worked out…everyone who wasn't hard-core but still bought these Jeeps was in some way influenced by the gaming campaign."

Intel's *Silicon Commander* is also demonstrative, though on a significantly more abstract level. Players of *Silicon Commander* operate a fleet of stationary and mobile robots, which basically represent desktop and notebook PCs. These robots carry out tasks for the player, such as gathering resources, but are besieged by viruses and other challenges familiar to any IT manager. Over time, players can upgrade their robots to "Pro" units (corresponding to Intel's "Pro processor technology"). These upgrades confer benefits such as greater security and higher performance, making it easier for players to achieve their goals. Rupal Shah, Intel's Marketing Director for Asia Pacific, nicely summed up the nature of the promotion: "With *Silicon Commander,* we don't just tell IT managers our story, we let them experience it for themselves."[6] Mariann Coleman, Intel's Integrated Marketing Manager for Asia Pacific, added, "Registered players spent, on average, more than 7.35 hours per week engaged with the game. Quantitative research found that 71% of respondents found that playing the game increased their product knowledge, and 72% viewed both Intel and the products more favorably." In other words, thousands of busy IT managers spent nearly a full workday each week playing an Intel advertisement.

Even *Froot Loops Toss* can be called a demonstrative (if relatively crude) advergame. What does it "teach" you? Mainly, that Froot Loops are tasty enough to satisfy even a monster. That seems like a message that could be conveyed via a fanciful TV commercial, but no consumer is going to engage with a TV commercial for as much time, or with as much attention, as they might an enjoyable advergame.

There is good reason to believe that demonstrative advergames can substantially increase brand preference and purchase intent, particularly when they enable you to directly interact with and manipulate a product (as did *Jeep 4x4*). Studies have shown that 3-D interactive advertisements can be significantly more effective than 2-D static advertisements, precisely because the former empowers consumers to actively engage with a product, whereas the latter is a passive experience.[7] This may be especially true in the case of complex products, such as mobile phones and laptops, as well as more sizable products, such as the Rubicon Wrangler. Given the cost and complexity of such products, it is easy to understand why consumers might want to interact with them (even virtually) before committing to a purchase. But, as the research on *Froot Loops Toss* demonstrated, even advergames that are only slightly demonstrative can be very effective.

Advergames as Two-Way Communication

In certain situations, the benefits of an advergame can go well beyond increased brand preference and purchase intent. Advergames, unlike so many other forms of advertisement, enable a marketer to form a direct relationship with a potential customer. At its most basic level, this may simply mean encouraging players to register with their names, e-mail addresses, and demographic information before they can play a game. While this is not the right strategy for many advergames, it can be very effective for games that are of particularly high quality, that are narrowly targeted, or that offer compelling prizes to players. Contact and demographic information can then be used to notify players about updates to a game, game-related contests and tournaments, and other information.

Players who specifically opt-in can also be sent other advertising messages.

At a more advanced level, advergames can also be used to study consumer behavior and even test the attractiveness of new product features. For example, in 2001 Nike released *Nike Shox*, a basketball advergame which enabled players to customize the color of their avatar's shoes before engaging in a slam-dunk contest.[8] Although it's unclear whether Nike actually studied the customization choices of its players, one can easily see how they might have used that information to forecast consumer interest in different shoe colors. General Motors understands this opportunity better than most companies. In 2007, it launched *Chevy Cobalt Labs*, a Web-based advergame that enables players to not only race against each other, but also substantially customize the features and paint job of their virtual Cobalt car.

Interestingly, *Chevy Cobalt Labs* requires players to carefully consider which features they most desire for their vehicle, as nearly every possible modification costs some amount of virtual currency. Additional currency can be earned through in-game activities such as winning races, or out-of-game activities, such as completely filling out your profile. By requiring players to spend virtual currency on the vehicle features they desire, General Motors has given consumers a great reason to do useful things, like tell the company more about themselves. More importantly, General Motors is learning something about real-life consumer preferences. After all, if in real life you care more about a car's spoiler than its wheels, you're likely to use your first allotment of virtual currency to buy a sweet spoiler for your car, and leave the fancy wheels for later.

Figure 3.1 Picking out a spoiler in Chevy Cobalt Labs (Reprinted with the permission of General Motors)

Making a Viral Advergame

One good way to understand what defines a good advergame is to examine a bad one, such as H&R Block's *Financial Match Quiz*. This game, which was launched on Facebook in 2008, encourages players to test their compatibility with friends by answering stimulating questions like "How do you feel about debt?" and "Do you know what tax deductions you qualify for?" Unfortunately, the ordinary person is unlikely to enjoy revealing financial problems or financial ignorance to friends. A good advergame, at bare minimum, should be *fun* and *viral* (that is, likely to be shared with friends and family). *Financial Match Quiz* attempts to exploit the popularity and viral nature of the stereotypical compatibility game, but is ultimately burdened with such dry content that it is neither fun nor viral.

In general (and unsurprisingly), the more fun a game is, the more likely people are to tell their friends about it, so the most important component of making a game viral is to make it extremely fun. Viral behavior can also be driven by competitive or collaborative activities, by the desire to achieve, and by the desire to share things with friends—especially when the act of sharing bears concrete rewards. These powerful viral factors merit a closer look:

Competitive or collaborative activities: This is an area in which video games excel. A game that offers compelling multiplayer activity, of either a competitive or a cooperative nature, will generally be more viral than the ordinary advertisement. After all, when a video game seems fun, people will naturally invite their friends to play it with them. Collaborative games are particularly compelling in this regard, since they appeal to both very competitive people (who will want help beating the game) and not-so-competitive people (who simply enjoy playing with others). A clever advergame might also use attractive prizes and group multiplayer competition to encourage friends to join forces and, as a result, maximize their prize-winning potential. Intel's *Silicon Commander* employed this tactic to great effect.

The desire to achieve: Many games use high scores and other goal-oriented achievement systems—for example, "complete this level in ten minutes or less and win a virtual gold medal"—to encourage repeat play. These features, when properly employed, can be used to encourage players to spread the word about an advergame. For example, when players achieve a high score, they might be given an opportunity to challenge friends to beat their score. *Nike Shox* enabled players to e-mail their high score and a snapshot of their best slam-dunk to friends—along with a link to the game itself, of course. The inclusion of the snapshot was a nice twist, and hints at the broader tactics that advertisers can use to make game-based achievement and self-promotion an even more compelling experience for players.

The desire to share good things: Video games—particularly those of the casual variety—occasionally enable players to give each other "virtual gifts." These gifts vary widely, from clothing for an avatar, to special food for a virtual pet, to allotments of raw virtual currency. Gift giving, though often motivated primarily by friendly impulse, can also be a self-serving act if it somehow benefits the giver in-game—for example, by rewarding the giver every time one of the giver's friends accepts a gift. This, of course, is no different from real-world promotional schemes in which consumers are rewarded with discounts or free prizes when they convince friends to try a product or service. Advergames that incorporate a virtual economy of goods and/or currency can benefit greatly from an effective gift-giving model.

In addition, the motivation to share user-created content with friends can be an especially powerful way to make a game more viral. When players have created content that they are proud of, it is only natural that they will want to share it with friends. Some advertisers even use contests to amplify the viral effects of user-generated content in advergames. For example, *Chevy Cobalt Labs* includes a feature called "Tricked or Trashed," which encourages visitors to vote between two user-created vehicles, "trashing" the worst of the two. As you can imagine, this provides great incentive for more involved players to refer their friends to the game and, in doing so, secure more votes for the car they have created. "Tricked or Trashed" logged more than 400,000 votes within a three-month period, many of which were motivated by the viral nature of the game.

Taking Advantage of Existing, Commercial Games

There is an additional strategy that marketers can use to create a compelling advergame experience: piggyback on an existing, commercially successful video game. A game that has already reached millions of consumers can be a very attractive platform on which to build. Fans of the game will be eager to acquire more playable content for it, and developers can use the game's preexisting technology to dramatically reduce the time and investment necessary to create compelling advergame content.

There are several ways to piggyback on an existing game, but the two most obvious ways are via "expansion packs" and mods. Expansion packs are a common strategy used by game publishers to increase the amount of revenue generated by a game. Additional playable content, which is often created for a fraction of the full game's development budget, is sold in stores or online to fans who can't wait for the next full game in the series. Mods, which we introduced in Chapter 1, "An Introduction to Games, and Why They Matter," are changes to a game's rules and content that fundamentally alter how you play the game—somewhat like the change from "tackle football" to "touch football"—though the alterations are often more extensive. Mods are generally created by fans and shared freely online, but there is no reason they can't be produced by advertisers as well.

One good example of this marketing strategy is *The Sims 2 H&M Fashion Stuff*, a content expansion that enables players of *The Sims 2* to dress their Sims with H&M clothing, and even design their own H&M stores. The expansion includes everything from mannequins to fashion runways and costs $19.99—a remarkable sum given that *Fashion Stuff* is little more than a glorified advertisement for H&M. Because *Fashion Stuff* is basically just a collection of H&M-related art assets that can be used in *The Sims 2*, it is likely that its development cost was relatively low.

Making Advergames a Reward for Purchasing a Product

One powerful marketing strategy is to create a very compelling advergame, then require consumers to purchase a product *before* they can acquire the game. The Burger King Xbox games, which we introduced at the start of Part II, "Games and Customers," are an excellent example. To get the Burger King games, consumers had to visit a Burger King restaurant, purchase a Value Meal, and pay an additional $3.99 per game. Fast-food franchises have employed this marketing strategy—most commonly with plastic toys and stuffed animals—for many years. But the perceived difference in value between a Beanie Baby and an Xbox retail game, which typically sells for $40 to $60, is absolutely tremendous to consumers. And Beanie Babies don't remind you of Burger King every time you play with them, whereas the Xbox games prominently showcase Burger King's characters and foods.

Burger King was not the first company to use advergames in this manner. In 1983, Johnson & Johnson released an Atari 2600 game called *Tooth Protectors*, in which the player had to defend a row of teeth from cavity-causing bombardments. Players could repair damaged teeth up to three times by invoking a special power, a tooth-cleaning regimen that included brushing, flossing, and mouthwash. If *Tooth Protectors* had simply been given away free, it would have been a great early example of a demonstrative advergame. But, in fact, *Tooth Protectors* was available only via direct mail order from J&J—eager gamers needed to pony up UPC symbols from J&J products in order to receive the game. Nowadays, J&J might use online registration codes instead of UPC symbols, but otherwise *Tooth Protectors* was years ahead of its time.

An advergame worthy of purchase must be a cut above the usual advergaming fare. Creating such a game requires close cooperation between an advertiser and a game developer. That can be a challenge for companies not accustomed to game development, but the end result is worth the effort. The Burger King promotion illustrates both the benefits and the risks of undertaking such a complex project.

Burger King's Pocketbike Racer, Big Bumpin', and Sneak King

In late 2006, Burger King began selling three games: a multiplayer racing game called *Pocketbike Racer*, a bumper-car game called *Big Bumpin'*, and an oddly compelling game called *Sneak King,* in which players must sneak up on hungry strangers and surprise them with a burger. The games were playable on both the original Xbox and the Xbox 360, with upgraded graphics on the latter console, and were all developed in just eight months. By all accounts, it's a miracle that the games were even finished on time, much less at any reasonable level of quality. Philip Oliver, the CEO of Blitz Games and a longtime industry veteran, doesn't pull any punches when describing the entire project, which was awarded to Blitz by Microsoft and Burger King earlier that year: "Burger King's ambitions for the games evolved substantially over the life of the project. If someone had told me 'You have eight months to write three Xbox games, which also must run on the Xbox 360, and can't simply be a port to the 360 but must actually look better, even though the 360 hardware isn't fully finished yet,' I simply wouldn't have signed up for it. That being said, I'm delighted with how it all turned out!" As well he should have been, given the 40% increase in Burger King's profits during the quarter in which the games were released.

Figure 3.2 Playing as the King himself in Burger King's Xbox game, *Sneak King* (Reprinted with the permission of Burger King)

Many factors drove the success of the Burger King games. Chief among these was the recognition by all parties involved that the games needed to be fun first, and serve as advertisements second. In Oliver's words, "Burger King wanted nothing more than to provide players with a great deal of fun and a lot of laughs—it would be pure coincidence that the games took place in the Burger King universe." Fortunately, the Burger King universe happens to be a rather bizarre and interesting place, thanks in no small part to the energy the company has invested into characters such as the King and the Subservient Chicken. Dr. Stacy Wood, Professor of Marketing for the Moore School of Business at the University of South Carolina, summed up Burger King's approach: "There wasn't a heavy sell with these games. Consumers thought they were getting a fun experience—not a sales pitch. For brands that have some kitsch value—some cultural capital—this is a great way to connect with consumers. When turning off the highway, their instinct to eat at Burger King, instead of another fast-food restaurant across the street, is going to be driven by a very fast decision that is influenced, in large part, by warm feelings like 'Burger King is fun.'"

Burger King also made the decision to sell the games at $3.99, an extremely low price for disc-based (as opposed to downloadable) Xbox games but, as it turned out, a potentially much better price than "free." By choosing to charge even a small sum, Burger King seems to have sent a message to consumers that its games had real value, unlike other advergames they might have played and been disappointed by in the past. Burger King further supported the games with a strong marketing campaign that included advertisements shown during *Saturday Night Live* and during NFL games. All this sent a very clear message to consumers: "There is something of value waiting for you at Burger King."

Furthermore, Burger King wisely decided to spread its bets by appealing to as broad an audience as possible. The company attracted "gift givers" and more casual gamers by pricing the games cheaply. It attracted enthusiasts by taking advantage of Microsoft's phenomenally successfully "achievement" system, which awards gamers points when they play games, and by building multiplayer functionality into two of the three games. And lastly, by creating three very different games, Burger King made sure it had something to offer any customer, no matter how narrow their interest in game genres might be.

The games were also so successful because Microsoft and Burger King had motivated and empowered project champions involved in the process. Within Microsoft, that champion was Chris Di Cesare, formerly Director of Marketing for Xbox. In Di Cesare's words, "The scale of the agencies and people involved in this promotion was immense. We're talking PR firms, ad agencies, online firms, game developer and publisher, and promotion agencies on both sides. It easily could have devolved into fiefdoms, but everyone checked their egos at the door and focused on Burger King's *very clear idea* of what they wanted to accomplish. Everyone fell in line because of

Burger King's passion for this project. However, the Burger King guys were total novices when it came to game development, so it became my job to translate their desires to the great many groups within Microsoft that needed to work together for this to happen. In other words, Burger King had an internal evangelist in me."

Finally, the Burger King games could not have come about without an experienced and reliable game developer. Blitz Games had a long history of delivering projects on time, and had also worked on several projects involving outside stakeholders and IP holders. As such, they were well suited for the Burger King project. Despite this, Blitz still encountered several serious stumbling blocks during the course of the games' development, learning hard-won lessons as a result:

Multiplatform development: To maximize their potential audience, Burger King wanted games that were compatible with both the original Xbox and the Xbox 360. However, they also wanted the 360 version to be more impressive than the original Xbox version; after all, the 360 had just been released and was being marketed as a high-performance, "next generation" console. Given the tight development time frame for the games, this took time and attention away from work that could have been put into additional game features and polish. Marketers should be aware that making a game compatible with multiple platforms—even platforms in the same line—can require significant effort, and should therefore budget and schedule accordingly.

Multiplayer challenges: *Big Bumpin'* and *Pocketbike Racer* both include online multiplayer action—an important feature of these games. Although online multiplayer modes can make a game much more compelling to consumers, such modes also make a game much more difficult and expensive to develop. Many developers consistently underestimate the difficulty of multiplayer development, especially on console platforms, and Blitz was no exception, though they ultimately managed to execute beautifully on Burger

King's vision. The lesson here: If you want a multiplayer game, make sure you reserve substantial time for the development and testing of that multiplayer functionality.

Different games, different assets: The benefit of creating three very different games was, as mentioned earlier, the fact that it enabled Burger King to appeal to different kinds of gamers and encourage multiple trips to Burger King restaurants. However, it also forced Blitz to develop very different assets (such as art and computer code) for the three games—time and effort that could have gone into raising the overall quality of a smaller number of games, or an equal number of more similar games. While developing three very different games ultimately proved to be a great strategy for Burger King, marketers who are seeking to raise the bar and stand out from competitors in the future may want to focus their budget on projects that are more ambitious in scale, but less ambitious in scope. As always, it depends on the situation.

Brand rules and restrictions: One of the biggest potential stumbling blocks for any game developer is something that marketers have total control over: the restrictions on how a company's brands can be used in a game. Failure to carefully explain and explore these restrictions at the start of a game development project can wreak havoc later on. Take the case of *Sneak King*. Blitz initially intended the game to be a Spy-versus-Spy-type game, with multiple Kings trying to out-deliver one another while laying traps for their opponents. After much design work, Blitz was informed that "there can be only one King." So Blitz substantially revised the design, choosing to focus on "king of the hill"–style gameplay; whoever captures the crown gets to be King. They were then informed that "you cannot 'become' the King." So Blitz adjusted yet again: One person plays the King, while the others play the remaining BK personalities, laying traps to prevent him from making deliveries. They then heard, "The King is too savvy to find himself in danger of any kind." And so on and so forth.

Some of the trouble with *Sneak King* was inevitable; it is impossible for marketers to predict every possible brand usage that a developer might propose. However, some of these brand-related missteps could have been avoided with clearer upfront communication. In particular, given the action-oriented nature of many video games, it was probably not hard to guess that "the King might find himself in danger." Marketers would do well to put time, upfront, into deciding and communicating what basic attributes of their brands are truly inviolable.

The Burger King promotion was expensive. In addition to the cost of developing the games themselves, Burger King had to pay distribution fees, promotional fees, and other nondevelopment expenses. In fact, the total cost of the promotion was ultimately many times the cost of game development itself, though it's worth noting that Burger King recouped a significant percentage of its costs by selling the games for $3.99. Given the effort and financial resources necessary to support an initiative of this scope, marketers wanting to emulate Burger King's success must be prepared to treat their initiative as a key one for their company. Otherwise, the risks of an expensive failure prove too great. Fortunately, as demonstrated by Burger King, the benefits of a well-managed advergame initiative are even greater.

The Three Keys to Success with Advergames

Among the keys to success with an advergame are the following: making it fun; "showing," not telling; and designing it to be viral (which makes it more cost-effective).

Make it fun: It seems so simple, yet marketers forget this all the time. A fun advergame is effective; a boring or frustrating advergame is not. Working with a proven and reliable game developer, even when that turns out to be more expensive, is the key to making a fun advergame.

Show, don't tell: Whereas most other forms of media are limited to declaring your brand's appeal, advergames can actually demonstrate it. *Jeep 4x4* uses gameplay to help consumers understand, firsthand, the benefits of driving a Rubicon Wrangler. But even seemingly difficult-to-describe products and technologies can be showcased via advergames. *Silicon Commander* is a grand metaphor for the benefits of Intel technology. The strengths of any brand can be represented through gameplay, given sufficient thought and creative effort, so whether you are advertising hamburgers or clean energy, there is a way of expressing your message in games.

Designing a game to be viral makes it dramatically more cost-effective: In many marketing campaigns, viral success comes down to luck—you put something out there and hope people spread it around. But when it comes to advergames, you make your own luck. There are many simple, concrete ways you can add viral elements to advergames, such as by giving players a way to compare their performance with that of their friends, as was the case with *Nike Shox*, or by enabling players to collaborate with and/or compete against one another, as was the case with *Silicon Commander*.

Endnotes

1. "Chrysler's 'Race the Pros' : Games Can Sell Cars," *Electronic Gaming Business* (August 11, 2004).

2. Yuanzhe (Michael) Cai, *Electronic Gaming in the Digital Home: Game Advertising* (Parks Associates, 2007).

3. See note 2.

4. Victoria Mallinckrodt and Dick Mizerski, "The Effects of Playing an Advergame on Young Children's Perceptions, Preferences, and Requests," *Journal of Advertising* (Summer 2007).

5. Ian Bogost, *Persuasive Games: The Expressive Power of Videogames* (MIT Press: 2007).

6. "Intel Seeks to Entertain Business Customers" *The Manila Times* (November 17, 2007), www.manilatimes.net/national/2007/nov/17/yehey/ techtimes/ 20071117tech4.html.

7. Hairong Li, Terry Daugherty, and Frank Biocca, "Impact of 3-D Advertising on Product Knowledge, Brand Attitude, and Purchase Intention: The Mediating Role of Presence," *Journal of Advertising* (Fall 2002), Volume 31.3, Number 3.

8. Hollis Thomases, "Advergaming" *WebAdvantage* (February 16, 2001), www.webadvantage.net/webadblog/advergaming-131.

CHAPTER 4

ADVERWORLDS, *SECOND LIFE*, AND BLURRED REALITY

According to Plutarch, Alexander the Great wept when he heard the theory that there are infinite worlds. When the king was asked what was wrong, he responded, "There are so many worlds, and I have not yet conquered even one."[1] Virtual worlds may make marketers feel some sympathy for Alexander—amazed by the rapid proliferation of these worlds, and confused by how to conquer even one.

Throughout the course of this book, we have already discussed several virtual worlds—*Habbo Hotel*, *World of Warcraft*, and *Second Life* for starters. While they represent just one portion of the video game industry, virtual worlds are unique in their capability to engage and empower people. Many large businesses and venture capital firms are pouring millions of dollars into new and existing virtual worlds. Disney and MTV Networks, for example, have both claimed to be investing up to $100 million in virtual world development—sums that ultimately represent a small fraction of the cash flowing into this space from video game publishers, well-funded start-ups, media conglomerates, and technology giants.

Adverworlds

Some virtual worlds don't merely contain advergames—they effectively *are* advergames on a larger scale. A growing number of these brand-centric worlds, or adverworlds, are free to players, and are primarily intended to keep consumers engaged with a brand, though they might also generate revenue via the sale of virtual items, real-world goods, or advertisements from partner companies. Perhaps more important, adverworlds enable fans of a brand to publicly express their relationship with that brand while keeping their real identities secret. Under the right circumstances, this can be a powerful and engaging experience. Imagine the fan of *Star Wars* who would like nothing better than to dress like Obi-Wan Kenobi and carry a lightsaber, but who is embarrassed to do so any day other than Halloween. A virtual world can provide an entertaining and perpetual outlet for such desires—not to mention a "working" lightsaber instead of a plastic one!

Among adverworld operators, few have been as active as MTV Networks. MTVN began by launching *Virtual Laguna Beach* and *vHills*, two worlds based on successful MTVN television shows. Users of *Virtual Laguna Beach* and *vHills* can visit locations modeled after those in the shows and can choose to wear a range of virtual outfits, including some that resemble those worn by stars of the shows. MTVN also screens television episodes of *The Hills* and *Laguna Beach* within its online worlds, giving fans a place to congregate and watch shows together.

Figure 4.1   *vHills* users chatting and shopping for virtual clothing
(Reprinted with the permission of MTVN)

Much of MTVN's focus is on engagement and the "emotional connection" its fans have to its content. Todd Cunningham, Senior Vice President of Brand Strategy and Planning for MTVN, shared the following insights: "We worked with Harris Interactive and MauroNewMedia to measure how emotionally connected our viewers are to *The Hills* on a love-to-hate scale. Viewers who had been exposed to our online efforts consistently proved more connected, and nearly nine out of ten users of *vHills* rated as being highly emotionally connected." Cunningham, whose focus is not only on enhancing engagement with MTVN's intellectual property, but also on improving returns for MTVN's advertising partners, added: "We can empirically prove…the more someone has engaged with *The Hills* through our online initiatives, the more likely they are to feel good about brands that have appeared within *The Hills* universe."

Media companies clearly have much to gain from investing in virtual worlds, which can prove to be powerful extensions of entertainment franchises. (Indeed, most media companies would probably not consider the virtual worlds that they are building to be "adverworlds," though the line is quite blurry. As Cunningham puts it, "Promotion and marketing and advertising are all the same thing as content.") However, media companies are not the only businesses playing in this space. In 2007, Levi's launched an adverworld targeting 15- to 24-year-old consumers in Hong Kong and China, with the ultimate goal of driving consumers to real-world Levi's stores. Users of *Levi's World* can acquire digital versions of the latest Levi's clothing, and can participate in daily events such as DJ music sessions, singles nights, and celebrity chats. By visiting the online world, users can also obtain vouchers that are useful in real-world stores. Levi's promoted the launch of *Levi's World* by hosting an online "red carpet" launch party, which was announced via in-store communications, print ads, online banners, and animated YouTube videos. Within 48 hours, more than 5,800 people had sent their R.S.V.P. for the event.[2]

Webkinz.com—The Latest Trend in Adverworlds

Like the Burger King games, Webkinz.com exists primarily to promote the immediate sale of a physical product. Every visitor who wants to take full advantage of Webkinz.com must ultimately purchase at least one Webkinz stuffed animal as the price of entry; many players have purchased far more than one. Activating the code that comes with a pet automatically results in the "adoption" of a virtual version of that pet, and grants you a large sum of virtual "KinzCash," which can be spent on food and gifts for your pet, decorations for your pet's virtual home, and more. But adopted virtual pets are not static beings—they require regular attention and feeding; otherwise, they become sad and ill. This, along with the enjoyable activities in Webkinz.com, effectively guarantees repeat visits.

Although excessive use of games and the Internet by children is a common concern for many parents, several commentators have found games like Webkinz to actually promote responsible behavior.[3] For example, if a child spends all her KinzCash on junk, she won't have enough left over to purchase food for her pets, which consequently become unhappy. Nor can she afford the more expensive and interesting virtual items in the game, which require real time and effort to save up for. (Webkinz features, among other things, an employment office where kids can get virtual jobs for virtual pay. Who says that child labor is an artifact of the Third World?) Webkinz has also been praised for its strict child-protection policies; for example, members chat with each other via preconstructed messages from chat menus—they cannot enter text freely.

If early results are any indication, adverworlds like Webkinz may be one of the most powerful forms of game-based marketing. More than six million people visited Webkinz.com in November 2007, up 342% from the previous year.[4] New users are given every incentive to continue purchasing toys, even though one toy is enough to secure entry into the Webkinz universe. Some incentives, like the

KinzCash bonus you receive every time you adopt a Webkinz, are fairly obvious. But there are other, more social forces at play as well—after all, children who play together online may inevitably come to desire the various pets that are possessed by their online friends. They might never have seen another Webkinz toy in the real world, but it is 100% guaranteed that they'll see all variety of Webkinz in the virtual world. And for *only* $11.99 each, they can have all of them...

Unsurprisingly, Webkinz has already inspired numerous competitors. Soon after Webkinz proved to be a success, Mattel launched BarbieGirls.com, an adverworld that consumers can fully activate by purchasing an MP3 player, which happens to look like a Barbie doll. After the user is registered online, the MP3 player serves as an electronic pass to BarbieGirls.com. Remarkably, the site reached three million registered users within 60 days of its launch. To put that in perspective, *Second Life*—which has received far more press attention—took three years to reach just one million registered users.[5]

As consumer interest in virtual worlds increases, media coverage continues to build, and technologies and platforms that ease virtual-world development become more prevalent, we expect a flood of adverworlds to hit the market. These worlds will be developed by media conglomerates, by game publishers, by start-ups, and by advertisers like Mattel and Levi's. Consumers will be faced with a bewildering sea of virtual destinations, most of which will share a very similar set of features such as avatars, customizable spaces, and virtual cash. Would-be creators of the next great adverworld should take note of this and plan accordingly. Adverworlds can be an incredibly powerful marketing tool; but they are neither cheap nor trivial to develop, and in the future they probably will not stand out without something unique to recommend them. "Something unique" may be a novel way of tying the virtual world to the real one—as demonstrated by both Webkinz and BarbieGirls. Or it may be a unique feature of the virtual world itself, such as the exclusive episode screenings that take place in *Virtual Laguna Beach*. In particular, savvy marketers will consider how their brand or product might be used to make an adverworld uniquely compelling, or uniquely attractive to a specific underserved demographic, and then build off of that.

The Four Keys to Success with Adverworlds

Among the keys to success with adverworlds are the following:

Foster social interaction: No one likes to be alone, either in the real world or in virtual worlds. Create interesting ways for your visitors to interact with one another, and promote in-world events that excite and draw people together. For example, *Levi's World* uses "singles nights" to regularly draw players together, while commercial MMOGs feature special one-time events—such as an alien invasion or an environmental catastrophe—to shake things up and force players to collaborate against a common adversary. Remember: An adverworld is a large and ongoing investment, not a one-time effort.

Don't start from scratch unless you must: Depending on the design, creating a virtual world from scratch can be extremely expensive. Fortunately, there are several companies that now provide platforms designed to ease the difficulty of deploying new virtual worlds, such as Metaplace and Multiverse. Although these platforms aren't right for everyone, they are certainly worth considering.

When possible, tie your adverworld back to real life: When implemented correctly, a virtual world tied to real products or places can be very powerful; the trick is to make the ties meaningful. Webkinz.com accomplishes this goal by bringing a stuffed animal to life online, enabling children to play with their toys in ways they never could before. Future competitors in this space might go one step further and make physical products that change state depending on events that take place in the virtual world. (For example, imagine a stuffed animal that audibly grumbles in the real world when its virtual counterpart hasn't been fed!) Any company with an engaging real-world product or retail presence can potentially take advantage of this tactic.

Give your customers a voice: As virtual worlds proliferate, the trend for freedom of expression in these worlds will only grow. Consumers will gravitate toward worlds that permit them to do more than simply consume content; they will choose worlds that permit them to manipulate, showcase, and redistribute that content as they see fit. Games are the perfect medium via which to enable this sort of behavior, as you shall soon see.

Marketing and *Second Life*

Second Life is a model of what a virtual world can be like when it emphasizes freedom of expression and community. As noted earlier in the book, *Second Life* is effectively a giant virtual sandbox filled exclusively with user-created content. Much of that content is created by private individuals working for fun, but a significant percentage is created by academic institutions, governmental organizations, nonprofits, and businesses of all sizes. Perhaps inevitably, most corporate presences in *Second Life* have been driven by experimental marketers seeking to learn about this brave new virtual world.

Although marketers have definitely made their mark on *Second Life*, the results of their activities have been mixed at best. Many organizations, such as Coca-Cola and American Apparel, have spent large sums of money building elaborate presences in *Second Life*, only to watch those presences quickly become vacant after the initial hype surrounding their launch died out. Other organizations, perhaps helpfully constrained by smaller budgets, have proven more ingenious and successful. For example, in 2007 Imax Filmed Entertainment promoted its screening of *Harry Potter and the Order of the Phoenix*, not by creating an entire "Imax Island," but by hiring two dozen people to work as virtual street teams for just seven days.

These teams handed out free virtual items such as T-shirts and 3-D glasses, which, when worn by an avatar, caused a *Harry Potter* promotional device to float nearby, turning *Second Life* users into voluntary viral agents for the film. The Imax teams also handed out a small number of free passes to the film, all of which were redeemed.

Figure 4.2 An Imax representative promoting Harry Potter within the virtual world of *Second Life* (Reprinted with the permission of This Second Marketing LLC)

According to Imax, more than 15,000 unique avatars engaged in conversation with and accepted promotional items from street teams during the week of the film's opening. Greg Foster, chairman of Imax, called it "the highest one-on-one branded interaction known to date that ever took place on *Second Life*," and added, "reaching 15,000 people in exactly the demographic you're shooting for over seven days is sort of hitting the marketing bonanza."[6]

There is no question that the demographics of *Second Life* are particularly appealing to businesses seeking affluent, educated customers. Sixty-five percent of *Second Life* users have a college degree or higher, nearly 40% have an annual household income of $90,000 or more, 70% are married or cohabiting, and nearly 60% have at least one child. Interestingly, nearly a quarter of *Second Life* users play as a gender, race, or nationality other than their own, and 11% adopt a different political orientation while in-world.[7] This implies a high willingness to experiment, as well as a desire to experience the world through different eyes—a useful finding for companies interested in relating to *Second Life* users.

Although relating to *Second Life* users has proven rewarding for some companies, many other companies publicly defected from *Second Life* in 2007. For example, in the first half of 2007, the NBA launched both a YouTube channel and an unrelated *Second Life* island. By July of 2007, the YouTube channel had already attracted 14,000 subscribers, and users had posted more than 60,000 NBA videos, which had been viewed 23 million times. The *Second Life* presence, on the other hand, had attracted just 1,200 cumulative visitors.[8] In its failure to attract a large number of consumers, the NBA has found itself in very good company. Dell and Best Buy, among several other major advertisers, have all found themselves to be the not-so-proud owners of deserted *Second Life* territories.

Why have these companies struggled to succeed? This question has been the subject of intense debate inside and outside the *Second Life* community. Supporters and critics have focused on four areas in particular:

Population size and growth: As of January 2008, *Second Life* had approximately half a million active monthly users worldwide—a number that had not significantly increased since July 2007.[9] Half a million users is not insignificant, but it is nothing in comparison to the active user populations of virtual worlds such as *Habbo Hotel*. Furthermore, seven months of stagnant active user growth is not generally the hallmark of a rapidly expanding Internet phenomenon. Given the very international nature of *Second Life*'s population, this leaves fairly small regional populations for local marketers to target.

User interface: Supporters and critics alike can agree that *Second Life*'s user interface is unattractive, unwieldy, and intimidating to new users. Furthermore, because the interface must be downloaded and installed before new users can enter *Second Life*, there is a natural barrier to entry that does not exist for more lightweight, Web-based virtual worlds. Some third parties have attempted to address this problem by creating their own Web-based interfaces to *Second Life*, but these efforts have thus far failed to make a dramatic impact on the population of new or existing *Second Life* users. Fortunately, this is ultimately a fixable problem—one the *Second Life* development team has claimed to be actively working on.

"Foot traffic": Critics have argued that *Second Life* simply does not generate sufficient "virtual foot traffic," not only because of a limited user population, but because *Second Life* has become so vast that visitors are spread extremely thin. A concise summary of the sentiment can be found in *Wired* Magazine, which reported the following anecdote in a widely cited 2007 article:

> As worldwide head of interactive marketing at Coca-Cola, [Michael] Donnelly was fascinated by its commercial potential, the way its users could wander through a computer-generated 3-D environment that mimics the mundane world of the flesh. So one day last fall, he downloaded the *Second Life* software, created an avatar, and set off in search of other brands like his own. American Apparel, Reebok, Scion—the big ones were easy to find, yet something felt wrong: "There was nobody else around." He teleported over to the Aloft Hotel, a virtual prototype for a real-world chain being developed by the owners of the W. It was deserted, almost creepy. "I felt like I was in The Shining."[10]

Supporters of *Second Life* have responded to these criticisms by highlighting successes like the Imax/Potter campaign, and by noting that many abandoned corporate *Second Life* installations were doomed from the start, since they lacked features that would make them compelling over several visits, and lacked staff to keep them alive in the absence of compelling virtual activities.

Supporters also argue that in-world foot traffic is just one measure of how many people a *Second Life* marketing campaign might have touched. A wide variety of popular blogs, such as *New World Notes, Second Life Herald,* and the official *Second Life* blog, regularly report on interesting in-world activities, and several extremely influential but more general blogs also frequently comment on *Second Life*–related news. These blogs collectively reach hundreds of thousands, if not millions, of consumers. There is also a wide network of third-party sites, message boards, podcasts, and social network groups that track *Second Life,* and a large number of video clips made in *Second Life* have been uploaded to YouTube. This loosely connected but fairly vast network of resources can, as of today, be easily tapped by a clever *Second Life* marketing campaign, though it is unclear to what extent that will remain true as time progresses. And while there is certainly real value generated by consumers reading secondhand about an interactive marketing campaign, no one knows how to measure that value.

Relative engagement: Advocates for *Second Life* have focused more on the length and quality of engagement that can be achieved in-world, and these arguments also have some merit. *Second Life* users are considered to be influential "early adopter" types, and engaging with them on a meaningful level may very well have significant benefits. A focused strategy of targeted engagement, as achieved by Imax's *Harry Potter* campaign, may be precisely the sort of in-world marketing that businesses should focus on, rather than more expensive private island-based initiatives.

Although issues of population size, usability, and engagement are all important, we find it odd that perhaps the most compelling aspect of *Second Life* has received the least attention from the marketing community. *Second Life* is, after all, defined entirely by user-generated content, so why has so much emphasis been placed on a unidirectional transfer of virtual goods and currency from businesses to consumers?

This is a point on which Wagner James Au, author of *The Making of Second Life: Notes from the New World*, fervently agrees. With characteristic enthusiasm, Wagner explains that while it hasn't received much attention, several companies have formed a more meaningful relationship with consumers—one focused on innovation. "The really cool companies are leveraging the fact that *Second Life* is a content creation platform, and that residents in there are building amazing stuff that you can use as a prototyping platform to come up with new product ideas, and to figure out what works in a market. The fashion industry has been really active in this regard, simply by paying close attention to virtual clothing that is being designed by consumers for their avatars. Philips has been working with users to design new appliances in *Second Life*, which they hope will eventually lead to real-world innovation. Steelcase, a global furniture company, is holding a design contest—entrants can create new prototypes of chairs and interact directly with Steelcase designers. And Pontiac did a really cool promotion in which they gave out virtual versions of their cars and encouraged *Second Life* residents to hack and modify them, which resulted in some really great designs." When pressed on whether *Second Life* users actually create usable designs, Au noted, "Some people like to create wacky designs, but there's a big industry for realistic items. One of the most popular cars in *Second Life* is the 'Dominus Shadow' and it's a straightforward, enhanced 70s muscle car."

These sentiments have been echoed by MIT professor Eric Klopfer, who notes that *"Second Life*'s real potential may be that of an experimentation platform…it's relatively easy for residents to build objects that others can use, sit on, walk through, pick up, and so on. That can mean anything from a hammer to a house to a landscape. And since it's also easy to share, replicate, and tweak creations, *Second Life* is a world of abundance for creators. That makes it an effective testing platform for trying out concepts quickly and cheaply."[11]

In other words, *Second Life* is an opportunity not to simply communicate to consumers, but to learn from them. As a venue for brand-promotion activities, it may very well fail to deliver the bang per buck of a property like *Habbo Hotel* or *Webkinz*. And as a platform, it may suffer from usability and scalability issues. But as a venue for consumer-led design and other bleeding-edge interactive marketing techniques, it remains the most prominent and exciting virtual environment to date.

Blurring Reality: Reverse Product Placements, ARGs, and the Future

For the past 30 years, games have been spreading across all manner of platforms. They started in arcades, became part of home entertainment, and are now found on cellphones and other portable devices. Games are becoming ubiquitous, and that is causing the line to blur between games and the rest of life. Two of the most intriguing forms of game-based marketing are taking advantage of this "blurred reality," but they only represent the beginning. In the future, the best marketing will combine real life and games in ever more intriguing ways.

Reverse Product Placements

There is one form of product placement which is currently quite uncommon in both video games and other media, but which shows how the game world can reach back into real life. We call it "reverse product placement"—the commercial translation of fictional products and brands *from* media *into* the real world.[12] Famous examples include Bertie Bott's Every Flavor Beans, a candy featuring flavors like pickle and earwax that was introduced by the *Harry Potter* franchise and subsequently converted into a real-world product by Cap Candy, and the restaurant chain Bubba Gump Shrimp Co., which originally appeared in the movie *Forrest Gump*.

The best video game–based example is a Japanese energy drink called Potion, which launched in 2006 and was inspired by a popular enthusiast game franchise, *Final Fantasy*. Potion was intended to evoke the "health potions" that players of *Final Fantasy* consume to restore their characters' health during gameplay. Two versions of Potion were released—a standard bottle, and a special bottle that included a *Final Fantasy* "art card." Although both proved popular, the special bottle sold out its three-million-unit run in an impressively short period.

The increasing popularity of games in general (and virtual worlds in specific) has created many opportunities for reverse product placement. Marketers seeking to launch new products can choose to spend tens of millions of dollars fighting mature competitors for mind share and shelf space in the physical world, or spend substantially less by first raising awareness within virtual worlds. However, this opportunity is not without its challenges. Marketers who fail to identify the right virtual environment—or who fail to apply sufficient ingenuity to the challenge of reverse product placement—will inevitably end up like American Apparel, which in 2006 launched a virtual store and promoted new lines of clothing within *Second Life,* only to close up shop within a year. Virtual experiences that are little more than pale imitations of real life, and that offer little emotional value or novelty to consumers, can never generate sufficient consumer interest to support a reverse-placement campaign.

Bertie Bott's Every Flavor Beans, Bubba Gump Shrimp Co., and Potion all capitalized on consumer affection for the media from which they sprang, and for the cleverness of the reverse placements themselves. These two attributes—a meaningful connection to a well-liked entertainment property, and an element of cleverness—are the defining characteristics of a good reverse product placement. And just as video games have proven particularly effective environments in which to embed product placements, we predict that they will continue to prove effective for the reverse.

Alternate Reality Games (ARGs)

Alternate reality games (ARGs) are another way that marketers are blurring the line between the real and the virtual. ARGs, like virtual worlds, are not quite games in the traditional sense of the word. ARGs are best described as collaborative, interactive narratives that blur the lines between reality and game. They employ a wide range of electronic and physical media to engage with players, such as Web sites, text messages, e-mail, real-world billboards, comic books, and staged publicity events. The end result is a storytelling experience that draws hundreds of thousands of people into an incredibly engaging puzzle-solving exercise that persists for days, weeks, or months on end.

Unfortunately, our description hardly captures the magic of a good alternate reality game. So please indulge us for a moment, and imagine that you are playing *Changing the Game—the ARG*. At 2:00 p.m. tomorrow, your cellphone might unexpectedly ring. A cryptic voice message explains that your help is desperately needed, and subsequently directs you to a "secret" Web site that will be available for only the next 15 minutes. You frantically run to your computer and load the Web site, only to be confronted with total gibberish. Finding yourself incapable of translating the text, you visit an online message board frequented by other fans of ARGs. An active discussion has already begun, and one fellow player has realized that the gibberish is actually just Spanish, written in reverse on the page. The translated text is revealed to be a note from a "government official," who has learned of a secret plot to topple the U.S. government and trigger a global war. Naturally, your help is needed to stop this from happening. The official's plea for assistance is accompanied by another riddle, designed to keep "others" from uncovering his subversive activities. This time, the riddle involves strange sets of numbers that, after some analysis, turn out to be GPS coordinates to a location in Venezuela. The community of players quickly recruits friends and family members, if not fellow confederates, who happen to live near the specified location in Venezuela, and before long a copy of *Changing the Game* is located in a mysterious black box. Unlike other copies, this one has a cryptic message written on the back cover, along with what appears to be a cipher. It turns out the book is just an elaborate front used by our "government official" to communicate with the masses while remaining undetected. The message and cipher are quickly scanned and uploaded for the entire community to see and use. And so the adventure begins!

Although we invented the previous example, many ARGs of similar and greater complexity have recently been launched with the primary intention of promoting a product or brand. This includes *I Love Bees*, a famous ARG designed to promote the video game *Halo 2*, and *Vanishing Point*, an ARG promoting the launch of Windows Vista. These ARGs have generally been revealed to the public in a subtle but highly viral fashion; for example, *I Love Bees* was first unveiled via a barely noticeable Web address, www.ilove-bees.com, that appeared at the bottom of the first *Halo 2* promotional trailer. *Halo* fans quickly picked up on the address, and began researching the mysterious Web site associated with it, which appeared to have been infected by a computer virus. Thus began a multiweek campaign that involved a number of remarkable challenges, such as one event that required players to locate certain pay phones all across the country and answer them at precise moments. (One person reportedly braved a Florida hurricane to take a call in a Burger King parking lot.[13]) Lucky players who answered the calls—effectively on behalf of the entire player community—were treated to conversations with live actors who carried the narrative into its next phase.

But of the many promotional ARGs that have been launched by advertisers, few have had such obvious, significant, and quantifiable impact as Audi's *The Art of the Heist*. In the spring of 2005, Audi launched this ARG in hopes of raising the profile of the A3 compact car, which was entering a very crowded market. *Art of the Heist* centered on a red A3 that was "stolen" from an Audi dealership. As the story unfolded, it became clear that the stolen A3 was at the center of a secret plot to pull off the "largest art heist in history."

Audi's goal was to blur the lines between the promotion and real life as much as possible. The company staged multiple live events at high-profile venues like the Coachella Music Festival and the E3 Gaming Expo, where actors appeared and engaged in tele-vised interviews. It published hundreds of documents, audio record-ings, images, and video clips that created a deep and compelling back story for the main characters of the ARG. It aired a national TV advertisement asking viewers to contact the company if they had any information about the "missing" car, and updated the audiusa.com home page with similar requests for public assistance. It invited players to participate in live missions (involving Audi deal-erships, of course) and rewarded them with invitations to parties and with Treo 650 cellphones.

According to McKinney-Silver, the agency behind *Art of the Heist*, more than 200,000 people became involved with the search for the stolen A3 in a single day. An estimated 500,000 people were involved in the search on an ongoing basis. Within the first few days of the campaign launch, fans created seven fan sites, one of which was "Top 10 Reasons to Play *Art of the Heist*." Visitors who were attracted to audiusa.com by online advertisements promoting the ARG devoted 34% of their page views to "buying indicator" pages—that is, car configuration, dealer locator, payment, estima-tor, and request a quote pages. This represented a 79% increase in qualification over previous launch efforts. Lastly, the ARG resulted in more than 45 million PR impressions, and generated more than 10,000 unique leads for Audi dealerships.

To call an ARG a complex undertaking would be an under-statement. Even the simplest ARG will, in general, be more time-consuming and expensive to deploy than many product placements and advergames. As such, when developing an ARG, it pays to understand what makes them compelling. Jordan Weisman, consid-ered by many to be the founder of this genre (he is also creator of *I Love Bees*), explains: "ARGs are the gaming equivalent of Woodstock—the big concert that everyone goes to for days or weeks or months, and then it's over. They're a social storytelling experience. There is no score. There are no winners and there are no losers. This form of entertainment is truly collaborative, and social standing is gained via contributions made to the community, not via competition for points."

Weisman is equally insistent about the importance of being strategically and financially committed to an ARG; in other words, doing it right, or not doing it at all. "There's a misconception that this form of marketing entertainment has to be cheaper. Well, it's not cheaper. A heck of a lot more effort goes into an ARG than a 30-second TV spot. You have to create a lot more content, and there's a much larger editorial process involved. But the benefits, as opposed to the 30-second spot, are the level of immersion you create, and the level of affection that a person has for the brand and the experience, not to mention the community that grows around the brand and the experience. Those things provide real lasting benefit to brands. And one of the great things about an ARG is that, unlike with a TV spot, you know how engaged people are. You know how many people visited your Web sites, you know how many people are participating on the message boards—you can quantify things."

We agree with Weisman's assertion that well-designed ARGs can be extremely compelling and engaging marketing tools. However, ARGs are a relatively new phenomenon, and as of yet there are few concrete examples of ARGs that have unquestionably boosted the sales of a product or fundamentally improved the perceptions of a brand. *Art of the Heist* is an inspiring example, but there are few others of its sort. Nevertheless, as the boundaries between the real world and games continue to blur, we expect ARGs, and other as-yet-uninvented types of entertainment, to become increasingly important tools for marketers.

The Three Keys to Success with ARGs

Among the keys to success with ARGs are the following:

Great ARGs are more than a series of complicated puzzles: A great ARG tells a compelling story, which makes a big difference to every participant, but especially to those who are more interested in simply following along than in solving complicated puzzles, or who have never played an ARG and might initially feel intimidated by the experience. The best ARGs will also include simple participatory experiences that players of all backgrounds and interest levels can engage in.

Put it out there and let them find it: Part of what people enjoy about ARGs is the way they seamlessly blend fiction with real life. Given that, it doesn't make much sense to formally announce the beginning of an ARG or to openly promote the marketing purpose of an ARG. Take, as an example, how the rock band Nine Inch Nails launched an ARG called *Year Zero* by selling T-shirts printed with their European tour schedule. Sharp observers noticed that random letters on the shirt seemed slightly boldfaced. The letters spelled "i am trying to believe," and naturally, as soon as people figured that out, they began flocking to "iamtryingtobelieve.com," which initiated the ARG experience. Nine Inch Nails maintained the mystery throughout *Year Zero*'s life cycle, never revealing to fans where the ARG was going or how it would end. Fans reported that this was perhaps the most exciting aspect of the entire experience.[14]

Make it a true multimedia experience: In general, an ARG will prove more engaging if it takes advantage of multiple mediums, such as postcards, e-mail, realistic-looking news articles leaked through blogs and media outlets, billboards, phone calls, radio broadcasts, YouTube videos, print advertisements, and the backsides of T-shirts. This helps blur the lines between reality and the game and keeps players on their toes.

Endnotes

1. Plutarch, "Morales," translated by Arthur Richard Shilleto (London, 1898), IV from Project Guttenberg, http://www.gutenberg.org/files/23639/23639-8.txt, paraphrase from the annotations of Wilmot H. McCutchen, "15 Ancient Greek Heroes from Plutarch's Lives" (2000), available at http://www.e-classics.com.

2. Dawn Anfuso, "Levi's Launches International Virtual Worlds," *iMedia Connections* (October 23, 2007), www.imediaconnection.com/news/17092.asp.

3. Kathleen Deveny, "Financial Tips From Fluffy," *Newsweek* (March 10, 2008), www.newsweek.com/id/117928; and Christine Hurt, "Webkinz: The Sims for Kids," *The Conglomerate* (April 27, 2007), www.theconglomerate.org/2007/04/webkinz_the_sim.html.

4. Brooks Barnes, "Web Playgrounds of the Very Young," *The New York Times* (December 31, 2007).

5. Duncan Riley, "Could Barbie Girls Become the Largest Virtual World?" *TechCrunch* (July 15, 2007), www.techcrunch.com/2007/07/15/could-barbie-girls-become-the-largest-virtual-world/.

6. "'Phoenix' soars into Second Life," *The Hollywood Reporter* (August 3, 2007), www.hollywoodreporter.com/hr/content_display/news/e3i7ba34c61f8b25ae278d c647741c6f273.

7. Wagner James Au, "Surveying Second Life," *New World Notes* (April 30, 2007), http://nwn.blogs.com/nwn/2007/04/second_life_dem.html.

8. Frank Rose, "How Madison Avenue Is Wasting Millions on a Deserted Second Life," *Wired* (July 24, 2007), www.wired.com/techbiz/media/magazine/ 15-08/ff_sheep.

9. Wagner James Au, "Peaking Paradox: Why Does SL's Peak Concurrency Grow While Monthly User Numbers Remain Plateaued?" *New World Notes* (February 2008), http://nwn.blogs.com/nwn/2008/02/peaking-paradox.html.

10. See note 8.

11. Steve Mollman, "Second Life's 2nd Value: Testing Ideas," *CNN Digital Business* (September 23, 2007), http://edition.cnn.com/2007/BUSINESS/09/16/second.life/.

12. David Edery, "Reverse Product Placement in Virtual Worlds," *Harvard Business Review* (December 2006).

13. Frank Rose, "Secret Websites, Coded Messages: The New World of Immersive Games," *Wired* (December 20, 2007), www.wired.com/entertainment/music/magazine/16-01/ff_args.

14. Ibid.

PART III

GAMES AND EMPLOYEES

The SUV lost control and rolled over, flipping five times before coming to a rest on the side of the highway. Paxton Galvanek quickly stopped his car and ran across the road to see if he could help while his wife called 911. He found two men inside the overturned vehicle. One was only slightly hurt, but the other was bleeding from a severe head wound and had lost two fingers. Unless someone helped the injured man, he was likely to die, and Galvanek had never taken first-aid training. However, he had played *America's Army*, a video game that requires you to learn basic medical procedures in a virtual classroom before healing other injured players in the game. Recalling the ways that he had dealt with injuries in the game, Galvanek properly treated the victims' wounds until help arrived. He later wrote, "I have received no prior medical training and can honestly say that because of the training and presentations within *America's Army*, I was able to help and possibly save the injured men. As I look back on the events of that day, the training that I received in the *America's Army* video game keeps coming to mind."[1]

The life saved by Galvanek is tangible evidence of the power of games to educate. Games can provide a new way to engage employees while teaching them, even when they are not aware that they are being taught. Far-sighted companies are using games to recruit, train, motivate, and make employees more productive. This section of the book explores these examples in greater detail. Chapter 5, "Better

Employees through Gaming," is an overview of games and employee training in general. Chapter 6, "Three Skills for an Interconnected World," focuses on three specific, vital skills that video games can teach. Finally, Chapter 7, "Games and Recruiting," explains how companies are using games to find and recruit the best employees.

Before we begin, there are a couple of important issues worth mentioning. First, there has been a lot of emphasis in recent years on gaming as it relates to "generation gaps." The basic idea is that young people, sometimes called millennials or Generation Y, have grown up with video games, and therefore think in different ways than older people. Some argue that, as a result, games are primarily a way of relating to younger workers, rather than a tool that can be leveraged across an entire organization. Although catering to young workers can be important, it is also important to recognize that games are not the exclusive domain of the young, as discussed in Chapter 1, "An Introduction to Games, and Why They Matter."

Young employees may initially relate more easily to games in the workplace, but that does not mean that games are more useful to them. In fact, one intriguing study of a game designed for NYU Medical School suggests that the opposite could be true. The game, known as *Pete Armstrong*, was designed to improve the attitude of young people toward those with disabilities. Interestingly enough, researchers found that the game had the greatest effect on people with the *least* game-playing experience.[2] Furthermore, the relatively scarce research that exists on games and business training has not found a strong link between age and ability to learn from games, despite speculation to the contrary.[3] It is therefore best to avoid delving too deeply into generational psychology, and instead to focus on how video games can benefit *everybody* within an organization.

The second issue we want to touch on is that, although most of our examples are from the commercial world, there are also many examples drawn from the military. Why? Because the military, in the words of BBN Division Scientist and game researcher Bill Ferguson, is "the only large organization in the country that spends 90% of its time training," and that is willing to be open about the results. The links between industry, the military, and games for entertainment are quite extensive. The very first business games, developed by the RAND Corporation in the 1950s, were direct descendants of an early military war game called *Kriegspiel*, which was used to teach the Prussian army in the 19th century.

Similarly, the first sophisticated flight simulator, the Link Trainer, was used to train half a million World War II fighter pilots. However, when the trainer was first introduced in 1932, the U.S. government owned only a single simulator—but there were 50 at Coney Island and other amusement parks.[4] Today, some companies that make simulators for the military later repackage them as games for both entertainment use and business training. This tight connection between the military, industry, and games is certainly not without its critics, with some branding it the "military-industrial-entertainment complex." But though the military has been more open about its use of games than most other organizations, it is just one of many that are using games for training.

Endnotes

1. B. Lindsey, "Gamer Uses Virtual Medic Training to Help Save a Life," *GamerNode* (2008), http://www.gamernode.com/news/5647-gamer-uses-virtual-medic-training-to-help-save-a-life/index.html.

2. D. Jacobson, "Pete Armstrong" (2006), http://bigfun.net/pete/.

3. J. Kenworthy, and A. Wong, "Developing Managerial Effectiveness: Assessing and Comparing the Impact of Development Programmes Using a Management Simulation or a Management Game," *Developments in Business Simulations and Experiential Learning* 32 (2005).

4. J. D. Derian, "All But War is Simulation" in *Rethinking Geopolitic*, Ed. Simon Dalby and Geroid O. Tuathail (Routledge: 1998).

CHAPTER 5

BETTER EMPLOYEES THROUGH GAMING

Employee training might be the best business expense, at least in terms of pure return on investment. According to the latest research, returns on training range from 7% to 50% per dollar spent, and more detailed case studies report even higher numbers, with returns of 100% to 200% on investment.[1] With results like these, it is not surprising that spending on corporate training exceeded $46 billion in 2006 in the U.S. alone.[2] However, a remarkably small percentage of that sum was spent on games and training—something on the order of $150 million.[3]

We suspect that this amount is so small because many educational and training games have developed a deservedly poor reputation. The problem with educational games started in the early days of the video game industry. Back then, few people took games seriously, so they were often ignored or downplayed by educators. The few educational games that were developed tended to be crude one-off efforts that were incredibly unsophisticated when compared to games built purely for entertainment purposes. Mediocre educational games rarely inspired students, but because they were the only games available to forward-thinking teachers, they were commonly used in classrooms and universities.

It was these rather primitive games that ended up being studied by early researchers who sought to understand the potential power of games for teaching, and it was unsurprising when they found only weak evidence of a meaningful impact on learning. These results discouraged educational game development, and the cycle continued. The things that games were best at—turning work into fun while encouraging experimentation—were increasingly ignored in favor of dry instructional material with quiz-show elements, or "games" that involved choosing a company's value statement out of four possibilities.

The Name of the Game

In many companies, "game" is a bad word. At the most paranoid organizations, people who type the word "game" into a search engine are likely to get a visit from HR asking them why they are wasting company time. The result has been a widespread effort among corporate training types to avoid using the word "game" at any cost. Even "serious game," the term preferred by many industry experts, is being displaced by euphemisms such as "immersive learning system" or "lightweight experiential learning platform." We choose to call a game a game, but we forgive you for using euphemisms if you need them at your company.

Trainers and researchers have invented many terms that refer to the various categories of games used for training. These are based on analyses of game types, goals, instructional methods, and other features. Though these categories are useful to academics and training professionals, they are much less helpful to managers. If you want to learn the details of various training game types, some resources are available at www.ChangingTheGameBook.com.

Hints as to the usefulness of games for teaching have been around for decades, however. Military trainers, as well as 1980s Tom Cruise fans, have long had a powerful example of the value of competitive games for training. The story begins in Vietnam, where, as the Vietnam War started, American fighter pilots were feeling extremely confident, and for good reason. During the war in Korea, American pilots had performed brilliantly against North Korean, Chinese, and Russian pilots in the first all-jet dogfights in history, achieving an exchange ratio of 10 to 1.[4] That is, for every American plane shot down, the Americans managed to destroy ten enemy planes. Vietnam, however, turned into a very different experience. Due to a combination of capable pilots, shifting tactics, and changes in aircraft, the Vietnamese were much more successful against their American foes. By 1968, the exchange ratio had fallen to 3.7 to 1.[5]

The fall of 1968 was marked by the beginning of a three-year halt in the bombing campaign over North Vietnam, and thus began a time when American pilots did not generally fly combat missions. In that year, the Navy commissioned a report by Captain Frank Ault to examine the relative failures of the air war of Vietnam. Ault's report focused on the training of Navy fighter pilots. From his report, the Naval Fighter Weapons School, better known by movie fans as Top Gun, was born in 1969. Top Gun changed the concept of pilot training, turning it into a competitive game, a simulation with real fighter jets between trainees and instructors who flew Vietnamese planes using Vietnamese tactics. The same training is now done using flight simulators, a technology obviously much less developed in the 1960s. And, while the Navy put its pilots through Top Gun, the Air Force also reviewed their performance in Vietnam. However, they ignored the training problem, choosing instead to invest in better missiles, improved planes, and high-technology cannons.[6]

The results of these two very different approaches became clear when the bombing campaign resumed in 1972. By then, Top Gun–trained pilots were in every Navy unit, still flying the same aircraft, while the Air Force had significantly improved their planes. The Navy's exchange ratio went up to 13 to 1, whereas the Air

Force's briefly plunged to an even 1 to 1 exchange.[7] It turns out that training, especially game-like training, really does help.

The story of Top Gun is reinforced by recent research that compares traditional training methods with simulations and games, though data on training is still notoriously difficult to gather.[8] In one recent study of management training, three separate groups of trainees were taught using case studies, realistic computer simulations, and a relatively simple management game. As might be expected, trainees enjoyed the games and simulations much more than the usual teaching. What was more surprising was that in improving six out of eight dimensions of management effectiveness, including the ability to lead teams and influence organizations, both simulations and games proved much more effective than standard teaching.[9] However, games can be more than a replacement for classroom exercises—they can also incorporate entirely new types of training that teach managers and employees to be more flexible, innovative, and effective.

Recently, people have begun to see the light about games and learning. More lifelong game players have entered the workforce, so the idea of using games for teaching no longer seems quite so odd. Additionally, various pioneers at universities and small game development companies have begun to show that innovative, yet inexpensive, video games can be made to train employees and managers. These examples have inspired others, and the reputation of learning games is beginning to improve. Educational games are finally delivering on the promise of transforming the way businesses train employees, and demonstrating the performance revolution that can result.

Fun Is Just Another Word for Learning

Educators have their own version of the Holy Grail, which is to make education so compelling that people voluntarily spend their time training even when they aren't required to do so. Games seem like a natural way to achieve this dream. After all, the best game designers know that for a game to be fun, it also needs to teach something—even if that "something" is relatively simple. The best games keep players constantly teetering on the brink of mastery, even as they employ new twists and challenges to force players to rethink the lessons they have already learned. As one famous game designer noted, "Fun is just another word for learning"—a sentiment echoed by many other well-known creators of games.[10]

At the very least, all good games teach players how to accomplish the goals of the game. *Grand Theft Auto* teaches you not to commit crimes when police are in the vicinity, otherwise you'll find yourself in trouble. *The Sims* teaches you how to keep your little simulated people fed, housed, and happy. *Solitaire* teaches you that moving a card on top of an ace isn't always the best strategy. All games teach—they simply may not teach something that is immediately useful outside the game.

From this perspective, it seems as though making games that are both fun and educational should be easy. And, in fact, some games that were designed primarily to be fun, such as a famous strategy game called *Civilization*, have unintentionally turned out to be quite useful educational tools.[11] (*Civilization* exposes players to a wide variety of historical facts while keeping them fully engaged in creating a global empire.) But designing a game that is primarily intended to be educational, yet is still fun, has turned out to be much more challenging.

Faced with this difficulty, trainers and educators tried a different approach. They began using games to spice up boring activities like typing, vocabulary learning, and basic mathematical problem solving. In these games, repetition and memorization were the primary learning mechanism. For example, a game called *Typing of the Dead* requires players to quickly type words in order to kill advancing zombie hordes. A more famous example is *Where in the World*

Is Carmen Sandiego?, which challenges players to hunt down a fugitive by looking up clues in an almanac (for example, "The thief dropped a feather from a pink cockatoo—where can we find those?"). The corporate equivalent of these games is the "game show" inserted into the middle of an online training session, in which trainees attempt to achieve a high score by answering questions about a company's confidentiality policy.

This approach to fusing learning and games has resulted in consistently mediocre experiences over the years. Though *Typing of the Dead* and *Where in the World Is Carmen Sandiego?* can indeed teach people typing or geography, there is little evidence that they do so any better than traditional teaching methods, or that they are significantly more interesting than time spent in a classroom.[12] And, in attempting to merge games and learning in a rather crude way, most games in this genre sacrifice almost all of the fun of games.

The Cost of Training Games

When you ask a random corporate trainer what he thinks the biggest barrier to using games might be, he will inevitably mention cost. In fact, according to training association the eLearning Guild, 70% of corporate trainers think the costs of development are going to be prohibitive.[13] Fortunately, they are wrong. The eLearning Guild survey looked at more than 50 games built for corporate training, and found the average project cost to be $75,000, with about half the projects coming in below $50,000. Based on the Guild's calculations, that equals a median cost per learner of just $102.08, and an average cost of $284.53—a remarkable bargain in the world of training.

Of course, these less expensive games are likely to be much less sophisticated than their commercial counterparts. However, as noted earlier in this book,

---

many polished commercial games support mods (modifications) that can make it relatively easy and inexpensive to customize those games in a way that suits your needs. As a result, a wide range of game-play complexity and polish is within the reach of training game developers.

The problem lies not in the combination of games and training, but rather in the combination of *bad* games and *bad* training. They are bad games because they aren't fun, and they provide bad training because they don't offer any real advantages over normal classroom methods. They are, in the words of researcher Bill Ferguson, "20% fun and 80% learning"—80% as efficient as regular teaching, and only 20% as fun as a normal game, so no one wants to play them. As a solution, Ferguson has come up with an intriguing principle, which he calls "Eighty Percent Fun." Educational games should be 20% as "efficient" as a classroom, but should make you want to play them so that you *willingly* learn outside of formal training. Although Eighty Percent Fun is an elusive goal, it is far from impossible. Witness the Sun Microsystems game *Rise of the Shadow Specters*, which points the way to Eighty Percent Fun.

Eighty Percent Fun: Saving Sun Microsystems from Intergalactic Evil

Sun Microsystems has embraced the virtual office more than any other large company, with about half of its 34,000-plus employees working from home. According to Sun's Chief Instructional Designer, Brandon Carson, having so many remote workers can create problems in communicating the values and culture of Sun to new employees. Sun has spent considerable effort developing conventional training material, but because new employees may see their colleagues only a few times a year, a more subtle reinforcement of the company's culture and norms was needed. Sun also wanted to reach out to potential new employees and give them an understanding of the organization. Carson put it this way: "We wanted people to get a sense of Sun's culture, that we were a technology company on the cutting edge. We also wanted to get people interested in the company and talking about what we are doing."

Because this additional training would be optional, it needed to be compelling. As a result, Carson decided to try making a game to accomplish his training and recruiting goals. He reached out to Enspire Learning, a training design company based in Austin, Texas. Enspire traditionally focuses on the simulation side of corporate training, but eagerly took up the challenge of making something different. A key consideration was the fact that many Sun employees would be savvy consumers of games and digital content. Given that, it was important to everyone involved that the game come across as polished and professional—otherwise, employees might not take it seriously.

The Enspire team took their design inspiration from a game called *Abe's Oddysee*, a humorous game in a genre known as the "platformer," in which a player's character is viewed from the side and can move only in two dimensions while running and jumping between platforms. *Rise of the Shadow Specters* is set in the cartoonish Sol City, whose five areas represent the five divisions of Sun's business. The player encounters Sol City after it has been invaded by dark aliens called Shadow Specters, and is tasked with clearing each area of the city by finding and using certain artifacts. These artifacts represent the technologies developed by each of Sun's corresponding divisions. The Processor area, for example, gives the player access to the Multithreader, which, like its namesake in computer chip architecture, allows the player to have multiple characters on the screen at the same time. The Storage area, on the other hand, grants access to the Sectorizor, which lets players move large blocks around the screen, in the same way that data is moved on a hard disk. These gameplay elements, rather than the trivia questions about Sun that are also part of the game, best illustrate the way Eighty Percent Fun works. Playing the game requires people to acquire basic knowledge of Sun's business units and the technologies behind them. In doing so, players not only learn about Sun, but also absorb the idea that Sun is a cool company to work for.

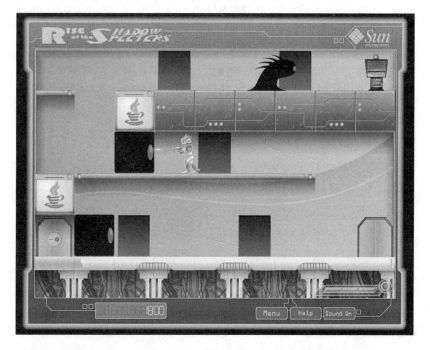

Figure 5.1 In *Rise of the Shadow Specters*, the player takes on both the forces of evil and the challenges of starting a new career at Sun Microsystems (© 2008, Sun Microsystems, Inc.)

According to Carson, the reaction to *Rise of the Shadow Specters* has been very positive, with several thousand Sun employees playing the game soon after launch. And, at a total cost of just $150,000, the game was relatively inexpensive to develop. But perhaps most important, several months after playing the game, we can still name Sun's divisions, and still remember that Sun's storage systems are responsible for 40% of the world's data—a testament to the way that fun can transmit learning, even to nonemployees such as us.

Although it's a useful example, *Rise of the Shadow Specters* isn't perfect. It was modeled after a very specific type of enthusiast game that typically appeals to a limited segment of the population, and the design choice made by the developers might not appeal to all gamers. As a result, it did not necessarily engage those Sun employees who, for example, don't enjoy blasting aliens, or who might have found the game too easy or too hard. The lesson here is that making a good, broadly appealing game that also teaches is extremely difficult, even when your primary focus is on making the game fun. Good training games require a combination of experience, an artist's touch, and the time and financial support necessary to really polish a work in progress.

In situations where training is optional, and where the goal is for players to absorb a few basic pieces of information, Eighty Percent Fun can be the best possible approach to training. But even in cases where the training goals are much deeper than this, fun remains a critical piece of what makes games compelling for learning purposes. Fun acts as the hook that makes people want to engage in a game, and it can get them to participate in training much more eagerly. But as much as we enjoy focusing on it, fun alone doesn't improve productivity or increase performance. To really impact the bottom line with training games, you need to understand the three most important things that games can teach.

Three Skills for an Interconnected World

Video games offer a way to intuitively teach people three very valuable skills that classrooms are absolutely miserable at teaching, and that even the smartest people have trouble learning on their own. Games can improve employees' ability to work in shifting and diverse teams, teach them to use systems thinking, and enable them to learn from virtual experience when real experience would be too costly or difficult.

Working in teams: The way a business's teams communicate may very well determine the success of that business. Research shows that the quality of teamwork explains almost half of the success of innovative projects in certain industries.[14] Teams in which individuals feel comfortable communicating with one another are more innovative, learn faster, are less prone to errors, and work better with other groups.[15] And yet, companies spend remarkably little time getting teams to work more efficiently, partially because such training is very hard, and cuts across levels of organization (try getting a corporate VP, a midlevel manager, and a new employee to all attend the same training class!). Video games provide an engaging solution to the problem of training teams.

Thinking in systems: The world is full of complex interrelationships, and we are very bad at intuitively understanding these relationships—especially in cases where the results of our actions are not immediately apparent. As a consequence, managers often fail to understand the systemic effects of their decisions. Study after study has shown that even in simple simulations, economists still create boom and bust cycles, government officials accidentally starve their populations, and experienced real estate and shipping managers find themselves bankrupt.[16] Games that teach systems thinking can help managers avoid these potentially catastrophic problems.

Learning from virtual experience: Learning through simulations and games is startlingly effective. Surgeons who use simulators to train are 29% faster and six times less likely to make errors.[17] Medical residents who use simulators to learn how to administer anesthesia complete their training 30% faster.[18] Truck drivers who practice in realistic driving games increase fuel efficiency by 6% and decrease their rates of accidents by around half.[19] Maintenance technicians who train on simulators score 33% better on examinations than those who don't use simulations.[20] All this applies to the business world as well. In one study, the teams of those managers who trained with a leadership game completed client assignments 22% faster than their peers, even six months after their training—the equivalent of an extra day of work a week!

In the next chapter, we will discuss in detail how each of these three critical skills is being taught using games, and describe some of the keys to successfully creating your own training games.

Endnotes

1. A. P. Bartel," Measuring the Employer's Return on Investments in Training: Evidence from the Literature," *Industrial Relations* 39.3 (2000): 502-524.

2. Bersin & Associates, "Bersin & Associates Announces Comprehensive Research Study of U.S. Corporate Learning Market" (2006), www.bersin.com/newsevents/06_mar_factbook.asp.

3. R. Jana, "Microsoft's Games Get Serious," *Businessweek* (2007).

4. W. J. Boyne, "Red Flag," *Air Force Magazine* 83.11 (2000): 45-52.

5. B. S. Lambeth, *The Transformation of American Air Power* (Cornell University Press, 2000).

6. B. Elward, *US Navy F-4 Phantom II MiG Killers (1) 1965-1970* (Osprey Publishing, 2001).

7. See note 5.

8. J. Gosen and J. Washbush, "A Review of Scholarship on Assessing Experiential Learning Effectiveness" *Simulation & Gaming* 35.2 (2004): 270.

9. J. Kenworthy, A. Wong, and D.C.E. Asia, "Developing Managerial Effectiveness: Assessing and Comparing the Impact of Development Programmes Using a Management Simulation or a Management Game," *Developments in Business Simulations and Experiential Learning* (2005): 32.

10. R. Koster, *A Theory of Fun for Game Design* (Paraglyph Press, 2005).

11. K. Squire and S. Barab, "Replaying History: Engaging Urban Underserved Students in Learning World History through Computer Simulation Games," *Proceedings of the 2004 International Conference of the Learning Sciences* (Los Angeles: UCLA Press: 2004).

12. R. Hays, *The Effectiveness of Instructional Games: A Literature Review and Discussion* (Naval Air Warfare Center, Orlando Florida 2005).

13. S. Wexler, et al., *Immersive Learning Simulations* (eLearning Guild, 2007).

14. M. Hoegl and H. G. Gemuenden, "Teamwork Quality and the Success of Innovative Projects: A Theoretical Concept and Empirical Evidence," *Organization Science* 12.4 (2001): 435-449.

15. A. C. Edmondson, "Psychological Safety, Trust, and Learning in Organizations: A Group Level Lens," *Trust and Distrust in Organizations: Dilemmas and Approaches* (2004): 239-272.

16. P. M. Senge and J. D. Sterman, "Systems Thinking and Organizational Learning: Acting Locally and Thinking Globally in the Organization of the Future," *Transforming Organizations* (1992).

17. N. E. Seymour, et al., "Virtual Reality Training Improves Operating Room Performance: Results of a Randomized, Double-Blinded Study," *Annals of Surgery* 236.4 (2002): 458-63.

18. S. Abrahamson, J. S. Denson, and R. M. Wolf, "Effectiveness of a Simulator in Training Anesthesiology Residents," *British Medical Journal* 13.5 (2004): 395.

19. F. Boosman, "Simulation-Based Training: The Evidence Is In," *Chief Learning Officer Magazine* (2007).

20. Ibid.

CHAPTER 6

THREE SKILLS FOR AN INTERCONNECTED WORLD

Teamwork Games: Climbing Mountains and Fighting Goblins

For two days in 2004, soldiers from the 29th Infantry Division were on the watch for flying goblins. To defend themselves, they had to rely on the spells of their wizards and the vigilance of their archers. Rather than being part of a secretive attack on Hogwarts, these soldiers were taking part in a military training exercise known as "Gorman's Gambit." General Paul Gorman was once the head of Southern Command, the Army headquarters in charge of Latin America. He had spent a lot of time thinking about how to improve teamwork in the military, and he came to believe that team skills could be taught in basically any environment. Specifically, General Gorman bet that storming a castle in a video game would be effective in teaching the kind of teamwork needed by soldiers during real assaults on fortified positions. This argument was put to the test via a fantasy-themed commercial game called *Neverwinter Nights*.

With the assistance of research company BBN, the Army modified *Neverwinter Nights* and designed a virtual playing field featuring two castles, each occupied by different platoons. The castles were connected by a cavern filled with devious traps, as well as a longer, safer path that wound through the landscape. Each platoon's goal was to take over the other platoon's castle, or alternatively, a number of "control points" scattered around the map. Each member of a platoon was assigned a fantasy version of a real Army role. The medic became a healer, with powerful spells that allowed him to resurrect the dead but with only a knife to defend himself. Artillery support was provided by wizards, capable of hurling powerful spells long distances, while the boots on the ground carried swords and chain mail instead of machine guns.

At first glance, the premise behind Gorman's Gambit seems fairly fantastic in itself. There is a wide gap between the deserts of Iraq and the elf-filled lands of *Neverwinter Nights*. But there is also a long tradition of using fairly abstract games to encourage teamwork and communication. Rope courses, paintball tournaments, and rafting trips have all been used to break the ice between teammates and encourage collaboration outside of the corporate setting. So why not use video games set in a fantasy world?

Neverwinter Nights ultimately proved to be an effective training environment. The researchers running Gorman's Gambit discovered that all the key traits of team communication—monitoring, leadership, adaptability, and many others—were demonstrated in the game.[1] Soldiers gradually improved these skills as the game progressed, despite the fantasy context of the game. Interestingly, many soldiers didn't even realize that they were learning anything from the experience. After the exercise, they insisted that they had not improved their teamwork skills, despite all indication to the contrary. Gorman's Gambit had accomplished its goal, but its players were too distracted to realize it.

Gorman's Gambit used a rather free-form approach to teaching teamwork—giving players a wide berth and allowing them to learn from each other in the process of achieving their goals. There is another game-based approach, which is to focus on very specific team problems that are hard to identify and correct. One such problem is that teams often prove dumber than their individual members.

This is caused by a phenomenon known as "process loss"—the opposite of the "wisdom of crowds." Process loss happens when teams fail to share information, get trapped by various conflicting goals, lose themselves in unproductive arguments, and fall into a pattern of groupthink. A game called *Everest,* designed by Harvard Business School Publishing and Forio Business Simulations, forces players to grapple with all of these issues and overcome them as a team.

Everest sends MBA students climbing up its namesake mountain. After watching a harrowing video describing the mountain-climbing experience, students are divided into teams of five and assigned roles with individual descriptions and goals, ranging from extreme sports enthusiast to the trip doctor. Over the course of the next hour, teams work their way up the mountain, and are faced with various challenges such as oxygen shortages, terrible weather, and sudden illness. In the end, the only way to win *Everest* is to work together as a team, share information, and adapt to rapidly changing circumstances.

As a game, *Everest* doesn't use the flashiest graphics to help people suspend disbelief. Players interact with a stylized map of the mountain through a selection of check boxes. The experience is rounded out with graphs and graphics that allow the team meteorologist to predict the weather and the team doctor to analyze illnesses. The game's genius is in its core design—it assigns slightly different goals and provides slightly different information to each player. The doctor knows crucial information about various diseases, but cannot act on that information if the marathon runner fails to report that she is feeling ill—a likely occurrence, given that the game encourages the runner to hide this information.

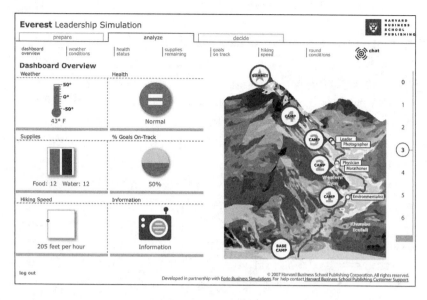

Figure 6.1   It takes teamwork to climb a mountain in *Everest*
(Reprinted by permission of Harvard Business School Publishing Leadership
& Teams Simulation: Everest, no. 2650, Roberto, Edmondson Copyright ©
2008 by the President and Fellows of Harvard College.)

These simple elements combine to create a very immersive and emotional experience—conspiracies form between the meteorologist and the photographer, while the doctor hides the fact that there is only one dose of aspirin remaining. Halfway through the exercise, any observer will be able to tell the difference between teams that are overcoming process loss and teams that have succumbed to it. The functional teams are productively calculating their remaining oxygen supply, while the dysfunctional teams horde information. Needless to say, only the functional teams make it to the summit. The result is a powerful lesson to all players, who learn in no uncertain terms what the cost of poor teamwork can be and the ways in which teamwork problems might be overcome.

In any game, players are rewarded for learning the rules of the game and applying those lessons properly. In *Everest* and the mod of *Neverwinter Nights* used in Gorman's Gambit, the rules are designed to encourage teamwork and punish failures to communicate. They are simple and elegant examples of how games can be used to teach the principles of good teamwork. However, as carefully constructed and compelling as these games are, they fail to take advantage of one of the most interesting recent discoveries on games and teamwork: Massively multiplayer games naturally develop and train leaders as part of gameplay.

According to research by IBM and start-up firm Seriosity, people who play MMOGs like *World of Warcraft* naturally learn some of the same leadership techniques taught to MBAs. Indeed, every skill expected of leaders in the well-studied Sloan Leadership Model was found to be echoed in online games.[2] This is because players of MMOGs learn to operate in challenging environments that encourage people to develop their leadership skills. For example, to achieve success in an MMOG, players must jointly tackle specific projects (i.e., "We need to kill that dragon") that require individuals to persuade and lead groups. MMOGs also help leaders with the difficult task of team selection by giving players clear roles and skills. A leader knows they need a teammate who can heal the injured or is capable of flying, and can easily see whether current team members have that skill. Finally, MMOGs tend to make incentives very clear ("The warrior wants armor, the wizard wants a staff, and everybody wants gold"), which makes it easy for leaders to align the goals of players on a team. Under these conditions, leadership emerges quickly and naturally, as individuals step up to lead a team, and then, just as rapidly, hand off control to other players as the situation evolves. This provides plenty of leadership practice to everyone involved.

In fact, in IBM's survey, three-quarters of all MMOG gamers surveyed said that the leadership skills they learned in games has helped them lead in the workplace. IBM's study concludes, "It's not a stretch to think resumes that include detailed gaming experience will be landing on the desks of Fortune 500 executives in the very near future. Those hiring managers would do well to look closely at that experience, and not disregard it as mere hobby. After all, that gamer may just be your next CEO." In both virtual environments built for training teamwork and virtual environments made purely for fun, the social and leadership skills learned are very real.

The Four Keys to Success in Teamwork Games

Among the keys to success in teamwork games are the following:

Teamwork games don't need to have anything to do with your business: In fact, if they are unrelated to your business, they may be more effective. That is because placing trainees in the role of wizards or mountain climbers may encourage them to take risks and communicate in ways they otherwise wouldn't. And, when implemented well, fantastic scenarios can have a huge impact on the degree to which a game is fun. It is also less likely that you will accidentally teach the wrong lessons about how your business works. Consider the students involved in Gorman's Gambit. If they were playing a game that involved a seemingly realistic scenario of storming a fortified enemy encampment, they would learn not just team skills, but also specific strategies to deal with fortified encampments. That sounds great—unless the scenario is inaccurate in some way. Then players might learn the wrong strategies, resulting in potentially devastating effects during actual combat. Building accurate training scenarios is hard; building fantasy ones may be much easier.

You need to know what skills you want to teach: Any game that involves teamwork will give people a chance to practice basic leadership skills, but more careful design is required to get the most out of any single experience. Do you want to teach how to handle conflicting goals? If so, think of assigning different winning conditions to the players, as was the case with *Everest*. Do you want to encourage teams to benchmark against each other? Try head-to-head competition, as in Gorman's Gambit. Whichever way you go, test your approach frequently and plan to tune the system to make sure it works well.

Instructors are required: To get the most out of a teamwork game, there needs to be an "After Action Review," or AAR. An outside observer familiar with a game and its goals needs to walk the players through what they learned, where they stumbled, and what they could have done better. The most complete AARs have game-generated success metrics and clearly delineated success and failure points; the low-tech versions use an in-game video and a clever instructor. Either can work.

Choose a punch line or a loop: There are two ways that a teamwork game can end. The first way is the punch line: "You all died on the mountain because people are bad at communicating. Let that be a lesson to you, and next time do things like this...." The second is the loop: "Good job, everyone. Now let's see if we can improve performance the next time around." Some games, like *Everest*, work best with a punch line, but it is simple enough to design a game that can be played repeatedly if that better matches your objectives. Just make sure to have clear goals for your game, upfront, or the design process will prove quite frustrating.

Experience Games: Crashing without Consequence

Clark Aldrich, a noted expert on games and simulations, likes to point out how terrible we are at teaching business skills. He argues that everything we rely on to teach, from classrooms and lectures to books, is inherently linear and static. Office life, however, is dynamic, and requires not just the careful use of a wide range of skills, but also the careful application of the right skills at the right time. Aldrich equates key skills like leadership to playing a piano, with "many things to do at once, but you also need to have the right timing, to play not too hard but not too soft, pulling lots of tiny motions together into a single effort." Becoming a leader, like becoming a good piano player, requires more than simple learning—it requires experience.

Simulations can give employees real experience, even if the simulations take place in virtual worlds. A study conducted by a Fortune 100 company examined people who had played Aldrich's *Virtual Leader* business simulator and attended associated training classes. Six months after using the simulator, trainees showed persistent and dramatic improvement in their leadership abilities. They had increased the number of client jobs they completed by an average of 22%, and reported significant increases in positive leadership behavior, and even larger decreases in negative behavior, according to a rigorous leadership assessment tool.

Many uses of simulators are pretty obvious. When the stakes are high—such as running a $5 billion nuclear plant or flying a $100 million jet—the use of games and simulators is common. But as an ever-incresing number of studies have shown, simulators improve the performance of everyone from truckers to doctors, so it is no surprise that simulators have found their way into the business world. Because simulations are the easiest types of training games to explain and measure ("It's just like real life, but you don't crash an airplane every time you make a mistake"), they are also the most popular and widespread way that games are used for training. If you meet some newly minted MBAs, chances are that they have used a business simulation. There are at least 200 business simulations that have been released, and they are being used by approximately 1,700 teachers in business classes around the country.[3] These simulations range from complex, multiday reproductions of corporate strategy, to simple company-specific games that teach customer-service people how to properly answer a call.

Many of these simulations are not games in the traditional sense of the word, although, when designed correctly, they draw on some of the principles that make games effective, including turn-taking and scores. The simplest simulations are essentially interactive spreadsheets that model aspects of a business and calculate the potential results. The player enters numbers into boxes representing, say, marketing expenditures or inventory orders, and clicks a button for the game to advance to the next turn. The computer then spits out the sales for the next month based on those choices, displaying them as another column of numbers, and, if you are really lucky, a chart—maybe even in color! As boring as that sounds, these kinds of simulations can be cheap and effective, especially when there is competition between groups of players to achieve the highest score. And, as you will see later in this chapter, interactive spreadsheets can also form the basis for games that teach employees how to think in terms of systems. Finally, even these relatively simple simulations have been shown to have a greater impact than standard methods of teaching strategy in business schools.[4]

Although spreadsheet-based simulations may draw on some of the basic principles of game design, they also sacrifice many important aspects of games in order to achieve their stripped-down form. They do not create a sense of immersion in a scenario, and with their emphasis on dry financials and clear-cut strategies, they can feel quite distant from the real-world experiences of anyone outside of the finance department. Interactive spreadsheets have their place in teaching the basics of strategy and operations, but they rarely offer the immersion, flexibility, and similarity to real life that can benefit the players of significantly more gamelike simulations.

If interactive spreadsheets are simulations that only accountants can love, Tycoon games represent the opposite end of the spectrum—games everyone seems to love. Tycoon games put the player in control of a business, with the goal of guiding it to financial success. Two of the best-selling PC games of all time, *Zoo Tycoon* and

Roller Coaster Tycoon, are representatives of this genre, and there are literally hundreds of such games, covering every industry from cruises to pizza delivery. In *Roller Coaster Tycoon,* the player is given a series of scenarios, such as "generate $20,000 a day in profit within three months." By placing rides and concession stands strategically throughout the park, hiring maintenance crews, taking out loans to fund expansion, and carefully setting prices while controlling costs, the player methodically works to achieve the scenario's goals.

Tycoon games use entertaining graphics and clever feedback mechanisms to make the player's experience enjoyable. In *Roller Coaster Tycoon,* if there aren't enough trash cans or janitors in the park, the negative results aren't merely reflected in a spreadsheet: garbage begins to visually accumulate in the park, and little simulated patrons quickly become disgusted and leave. Or, if there aren't enough benches at the exit of a particularly nausea-inducing ride for the patrons to sit and catch their breath, they may instead proceed to lose their lunch on the ground near the ride—dismaying other visitors. All the information about a business—the happiness of customers, the maintenance of the rides, the reaction to pricing or promotions—is communicated in a visual and entertaining manner that is both more intuitive and more engaging than a simple spreadsheet. People who couldn't or wouldn't touch a spreadsheet love Tycoon games.

Of course, commercial titles like *Roller Coaster Tycoon* are ultimately designed as entertainment, not as accurate business simulations, even though people may unknowingly acquire some business knowledge as a result of playing these games. Yet somewhere in between the interactive spreadsheet and *Roller Coaster Tycoon* is a game that accurately models a business but also offers an engaging and immersive scenario that makes trainees enjoy playing along. *Virtual Leader* is a trailblazing example of what an experience game can accomplish. Based on a leadership model developed by Clark Aldrich's Simulearn, it challenges players to lead in realistic office situations. Players are put in the position of starting a new executive job after being hired away from a competing firm.

Figure 6.2 *Virtual Leader* teaches real leadership skills in virtual meetings.
(By permission of SimuLearn Inc.)

The player attends a series of meetings in the first-person 3-D perspective common to many games. The first interaction they have is with one of the most powerful people in the company: the player's administrative assistant. The player wants to get new business cards made right away, but the assistant wants to complete some long-postponed administrative task, and, incidentally, to take Monday off. The player tries to accomplish his agenda by setting priorities, using techniques that can range from supportive to forceful. His computer-controlled co-workers have their own agendas, and react to the player's actions by looking bored, interested, or nervous, depending on the situation. As in real life, the straight path is not always the ideal one. A player who takes the time to get to know his virtual co-workers, and to make trade-offs between their needs and his own, will often gain access to important information and options that otherwise would have remained hidden.

What makes *Virtual Leader* interesting is how it encourages experimentation. After each round, the computer offers an assessment of the players' actions, telling them what happened as a result of their leadership. The reactions are visceral enough that when we were told that our administrative assistant had gossiped about how bad a boss we were, we immediately went back to try another approach. Playing *Virtual Leader* will not turn the ordinary person into an accomplished manager, but it provides an important way for players to experiment with and think through leadership styles. There is no other setting outside of an experience game where such freedom is possible.

Long-Term Experience: Through the Looking Glass with ARGs

Regular simulation games work well when the subject is something that is generally understood, and when the parameters of success and failure can be modeled by a game's designers. But how do you model the unusual and unexpected? A stock market crash? The sudden collapse of your key competitor due to an accounting scandal? A coup that topples a foreign government? A safety problem with one of your products? Any of these events could transform your business for years to come, and reacting quickly could spell the difference between survival and disaster. Responding quickly requires training. But unlike typical training, which focuses on the day-to-day aspects of a job, this training must help employees react quickly, improvise within limits, work in ad hoc groups, and use informal as well as formal channels to get things done. This is another area of great weakness for typical training and instruction. This is also where games can, once again, come to the rescue in the form of the alternate reality games (ARGs) first discussed in Chapter 4, "Adverworlds, *Second Life*, and Blurred Reality."

ARGs possess qualities that make them uniquely powerful for increasing the ability of employees and companies to deal with unusual events. First, ARGs are interwoven with reality—players interact with the ARG using the same tools that they use every day (e-mail, the Web, corporate software systems), and players are expected to play the same roles that they do in everyday work life. ARGs also unfold over long periods, allowing players to experience a scenario from the first day through final resolution. Committing a little time each day to an ongoing ARG allows employees to effectively train while they work. And, most important, a good ARG is both fun and deeply immersive, creating a believable world in which individuals want to solve problems and resolve mysteries. A good ARG can lead entire teams to voluntarily train themselves and push their co-workers to improve.

The use of ARGs for this sort of far-sighted training is still new territory, but one trailblazing example is *Dark Waters,* an effort by the Defense Advanced Research Projects Agency (DARPA) to train organizations in issues dealing with natural disasters and national security. Typically, a natural disaster would bring together individuals from many different organizations, all of whom would need to coordinate complex tasks on the fly. From the first moments of the disaster, the members of the team would need to handle a massive amount of information, deciding how to spend scant resources on a shifting and uncertain set of priorities. Training for this sort of complex and demanding scenario is currently handled with a PowerPoint presentation—hardly suitable preparation for a major disaster recovery initiative. Compare sitting through a PowerPoint presentation with the experience of playing *Dark Waters.*

Dark Waters began on January 8, 2008, when an 8.4 magnitude earthquake rattled the western coast of Puerto Rico, sending 25-foot waves racing toward the island's beaches. The devastation was terrible, and the military, various government agencies, and humanitarian organizations rushed in to help. Soon, more grim news arrived. On January 14, confused reports began to surface of survivors in isolated areas suffering from a mysterious and apparently lethal disease. Rumors of a biological attack began to spread, and panic gripped the island. On January 15, the hastily assembled 100 trainees of *Dark Waters* were deployed to the USS *Iwo Jima*, with the task of identifying this new threat and containing it. In reality, January 15 was the first briefing, in which players were presented with various realistic-looking documents outlining the "situation" on the island. Over the next 30 days, the trainees worked together for 20 or 30 minutes a day to gradually solve the mystery of the unusual disease.

As the players were drawn into this tension-filled scenario, they exercised all the skills that a joint task force would require, including teamwork, adaptability, and information sorting. But, according to ARG expert Jane McGonnigal, the players were also learning other critical skills that are especially important in an information economy. McGonnigal gives these skills hip names like "mobbability" and "emergensight," but they come down to this: the ability to intuitively handle working in large and fluid groups while using many different communication techniques. These skills evolve naturally as the ARG progresses, eventually leading to amazing, spontaneous feats of coordination, like creating entirely new code-cracking software for the purpose of solving a puzzle, or tracking down a single individual somewhere on Earth, using only on his picture and first name.

But ARGs don't need to involve complex puzzles in order to be effective, as one guerilla group of game developers at Enspire Learning proved. Working on their own time and on weekends, a team of four designers spent two months building an ARG, only receiving management approval to roll it out later. The game started when Tom Lainear joined Enspire as executive assistant to the CEO. Tom seemed like a real person, with his own e-mail, voice mail, mention in the corporate blog, and even a place in the official org charts. But Tom didn't really exist, and neither did a rumored new competitor to Enspire, "Cogniteach," or its CEO, Frankie Eastwheel.

Eastwheel began e-mailing various Enspire staff, trying to hire them away from the company. Over the course of the next month, secret packages, rumored break-ins, and the eventual posting of "stolen" intellectual property on the Cogniteach Web site roped players into a game world where understanding data security became a critical part of solving puzzles. By the time players had identified Tom as a thief, they had learned important lessons about security. Almost half of the people who played the game changed their passwords to be more secure and started locking their computers when they weren't in use. Perhaps more interestingly, in a company that specialized in more traditional e-learning, ARGs quickly became a favorite method of teaching. Four-fifths of players said ARGs were better than textbooks, and 59% of players reported that ARGs are better than standard e-learning.

The Four Keys to Success in Experience Games

Among the keys to success in experience games are the following:

Choose the appropriate level of fidelity: Realistic games, also called high-fidelity games, give more realistic experiences. This can be good and bad. If the realism does not accurately reflect real life, there is a danger that players will take away the wrong lessons about how the world works. Imagine a flight simulator that is photorealistic in every detail, but that allows planes to land at higher speeds than is safe in real life. You really don't want your pilot using that simulator to learn how to fly. Thus, the most realistic game is not always the best, unless it is an accurate representation of real life—and accuracy is difficult to achieve. Instead, it's best to choose a level of simulated detail that accomplishes your goals without going overboard on extra realism.

Make sure that players can tell the difference between things that are realistic in the game, and things that are not. This can involve using cartoonish art or a fantasy setting for the nonrealistic parts of the game, or even pausing the game when a player tries to do something unrealistic. Managing levels of fidelity can be tricky. For example, in one famous case, a military shooting simulator designed to teach accuracy did not require soldiers to reload after firing their weapons. The designers reasoned that no soldier could forget the need to reload their gun, and removing reloads enabled players to focus entirely on the highly realistic target practice offered by the game. What the designers did not anticipate was that players would begin practicing complex group tactics using the simulator. These tactics, which were later used in the real world, did not incorporate the time needed for individual soldiers to reload, causing considerable confusion. The lesson here is to pay careful attention to the skills that players will learn from a game, and to make all related aspects of the game realistic, while clearly marking nonrealistic elements.

Test, test, test: More than most other types of training games, simulations have to balance various factors, from fidelity to fun to learning. The only way to know if you are getting it right is to play-test your experience game with a wide audience, and leave time to make changes when necessary. The more you iterate, the better your simulation game will be.

Watch the line between work and play: Simulators without instruction can quickly turn into fun but pointless entertainment. It is sometimes more fun to repeatedly make a virtual nuclear power plant overheat, or to make a dam burst, than it is to maintain a perfect safety record. Or, as one of the authors of this book can personally attest, it is much more fun to ram into virtual buildings in an expensive and realistic armored vehicle simulator than it is to learn how to properly park. (The aforementioned author would like to apologize once again to the Army for the time required to reset the machine.) Guidance can come from the simulation itself or from an outside instructor, but guidance is required to prevent training from devolving entirely into play.

Leverage someone else's experiences: Lacking a Tycoon game that teaches game development (there actually is one, but, ironically, it isn't very good), it is important to reemphasize that developing games isn't easy, and developing good experience games is even harder. Creating a good experience game requires careful attention to what you want to teach, how the lessons will be delivered, and how you will measure the results. There are various resources available that discuss how to best take these necessary and sometimes challenging steps; in particular, see Clark Aldrich's *Learning by Doing*, which distills many of the lessons of building experience games into a series of detailed steps, more resources are available at www.ChangingTheGameBook.com.

Systems Games: Drinking Beer and Trading Stocks

If you want to see a group of businesspeople get really mad at each other—shouting mad at each other—have them play the *Beer Game*. First developed at MIT in the 1960s as a board game, the *Beer Game* is disarmingly simple. The goal is for individuals in four different roles to work together to supply beer to customers. The player who fills the role of the retailer is informed of the customer demand for beer each simulated week. In turn, the retailer orders from the wholesaler, who orders from the distributor, who orders from the manufacturer. The manufacturer ultimately chooses how much beer to make, and ships it to the distributor, who moves it along the chain.

There is only one piece of information that passes between each of these four players: the number of beers ordered by the previous person in the supply chain. Only the retailer sees what the customer actually demands. Each week, based on customer demand, the retailer places an order that only the wholesaler sees, the wholesaler writes an order to the distributor, the distributor orders from the factory, and the factory finally determines how much beer to make. Beer takes a week to move between each link in the supply chain, creating a delay of a few weeks between retailer demand and factory supply. The goal of the game is to minimize costs—each unsatisfied customer who can't get a beer costs the team $1 per week, and each beer left sitting in inventory costs 50 cents per week. The game runs for 50 virtual weeks.

It all seems so simple before it goes horribly wrong. The retailer quickly sells out of beer, and has to turn away customers for several weeks as the beer moves through the supply chain. Consequently, the frantic retailer increases his orders, while the wholesaler and distributor ship out all the beer they have on hand. The wholesaler, now also out of beer, orders more beer than the retailer demands in order to fulfill perceived future need. The distributor, in turn, increases *his* orders to supply an increasingly desperate wholesaler. Finally, the factory owner, facing huge demand, eventually brews a massive amount of beer, which creates a huge glut.

At the end of a typical game, the team has developed a huge backlog of unsold beer and racked up over $2,000 in costs, with many teams exceeding $10,000. The distributor, wholesaler, and factory decide to blame the customer, while the retailer remains strangely silent. Obviously, they reason, the customer must have had wildly fluctuating, unreasonable demands. Professor John Sterman of MIT, writing about the beer game, reports the typical player reaction: "It isn't my fault if a huge surge in demand wiped out my stock and forced me to run a backlog. Then you tricked me—just when the tap began to flow, you made the customers go on the wagon, so I got stuck with all this excess inventory."[5] To the players' inevitable surprise, however, it turns out that customer demand increased just once, and otherwise remained steady throughout the entire exercise!

What makes the *Beer Game* both a disaster to play and a valuable lesson is that it teaches the problems of dealing with interconnected systems. Even in systems as simple as the one represented by the *Beer Game*, individuals fail to account for the way they fit into the whole, and as a result, forget how their decisions affect the entire team. Volvo shows how these sorts of system errors can have massive real-life effects.[6] In the 1990s, Volvo made a mistake in its forecasting, building too many green cars that they couldn't seem to sell. The marketing group at Volvo jumped on the problem by offering special deals on green cars, and the automobiles finally began to move. The supply chain management group hadn't been part of the decision to put the special offer in place, and therefore saw only the results—green cars were starting to sell! So they quickly notified the factory to increase the number of green cars in production. The result was that Volvo was left with a huge backlog of green cars that they couldn't sell.

System-level thinking is notoriously difficult to teach because it involves unintended consequences and complex interrelationships. Yet, with an exponentially increasing number of interdependencies, businesses require system-level thinking from all their employees. Michael Bean of Forio pointed out that just such a failure among individual employees to understand systems cost Cisco $2.2 billion and 8,500 jobs in 2001. Even as the dot-com boom ended, demand for Cisco's products seemed to be skyrocketing. In reality, that demand did not truly exist, but Cisco's salespeople were nevertheless continuing to increase their sales forecasts. The reason was, according to a supplier, that "salespeople don't want to be caught without supply, so they make sure they have supply by forecasting more sales than they expect. Procurement needs 100 of a part, but they know if they ask for 100, they'll get 80. So they ask for 120 to get 100."[7] Cisco's manufacturing staff saw the inflated order numbers and jumped to the wrong conclusions, causing a disaster when the market finally came crashing down.

Companies need a new way to address the increasing interconnectedness of their operations at a time when the entirely reasonable assumptions of a few salespeople can turn into billions of dollars in losses. The way to do this is to get every employee to understand how their actions play a role in the success or failure of the entire organization. Fortunately, this sort of systems thinking is not just found in the *Beer Game*, it is an integral part of some of the best-selling video games of all time. *SimCity*, for example, is a well-known city-planning franchise that has been both a perennial member of the bestseller charts and a feature of classrooms.

Figure 6.3 Balancing the complex system of municipal services, budgets, and regulations that are needed to grow a metropolis is fun in *SimCity* (*SimCity, The Sims, and The Sims 2* ™ and © of Electronic Arts Inc. Used with permission.)

SimCity is a remarkably undirected game, with few overall goals except for the player's desire to build the city that they want to build. To accomplish this task, the player must balance a seemingly endless list of priorities, including water, power, education, transportation, budget, crime rates, industrial zoning, and more. On paper (and at city planning offices!), these factors seem overwhelming, and require half a dozen analysts to make a single zoning decision. In *SimCity*, however, the nature of the system becomes so transparent that children in grade school find the game easy to use. ("If I put a residential area by the industrial zone, it will have lower property values, but its residents will have a shorter commute and will contribute less to traffic, so I can spend less on roads and more on things that increase property values, like parks and recreational areas.") The consequences of every action are reflected graphically in the game—for example, roads become choked with traffic if players fail to supply sufficient transportation options for a growing city.

Another game that teaches the complexity of systems, but for a much more serious purpose, is *Peacemaker*. In *Peacemaker*, the goal of the player is nothing less than to solve the Israeli-Palestinian conflict by playing the role of either the Israeli Prime Minister or the head of the Palestinian Authority. Players are challenged to navigate a way through violence and complex diplomatic issues. In doing so, they learn a great deal about the situation in the Middle East. As one of the game's designers, Israeli Asi Burak, explained, "People get very engaged. They really try very hard to get a solution. Even after one hour or two hours, they'd come to me and say, you know, I know more about the conflict than when I've read newspapers for ten years."[8] *SimCity* and *Peacemaker* demonstrate how games can make the complex world of systems easier to understand. If the salespeople at Cisco or the marketing managers at Volvo had a chance to play *SimCisco* or *SimVolvo*, they might have understood the way that even minor changes in the way they did business could affect the entire organization.

Uptick, designed by Harvard Business School Professors Joshua Coval and Erik Stafford, is an example of how a clever systems-level game can teach the counterintuitive rules of the financial system and stock market. Professor Stafford explains that the problem with teaching finance is that the market works through the effects of large groups of people. This is often very hard to intuitively understand, since "you can spend years studying finance and just know the details. If you can understand these group effects, then you can understand any setting that you go to. That's the real secret behind finance, and what we're poorly equipped to teach otherwise."

Business schools and financial institutions around the world teach the same basic equations about how the markets work, but they often don't give the students an understanding of how the system actually functions. As a result, students often come to think that the lessons they are learning are only academic ideals, and that in the real world they would be able to figure out ways to manipulate the market. *Uptick* changes their minds quickly. Using accurate historical data about the stock market, as well as the students' desire to get the highest score possible, *Uptick* creates a stock market in miniature, with students and computer-run traders each given a sum of money to invest. Students are essentially pitted against each other in a competition to earn the highest returns, and they quickly rediscover in practice all the equations they learned in theory, and get a very visceral sense of how the market works.

Professor Stafford says this isn't always to everyone's liking: "The people who want to learn finance can now learn finance at a level they never thought possible, and they think it is the best class they have ever taken. They put 20 hours a week in, and at the end they have learned five different trading strategies. The others are forced to compete with these people, and they lose. People who go into professional finance management are the psychos who love it and spend every waking minute on it." In essence, the rest of the class serves as the regular investors, while the Wall Street types figure out how to make money off them. By understanding how the market works by being part of it, students get a better sense of the main lesson of any finance class: "It is pretty damn difficult to make money in financial markets"—even if you are a Harvard Business School graduate.

Even experienced professionals can benefit from systems-level games, because they rarely have a chance to think about the entirety of the systems in which they operate. For example, the Chartered

Financial Analyst Institute sends some of the best minds in finance to classes in which *Uptick* is featured. Rather than avoiding the mistakes that MBA students encounter, these financial geniuses find themselves falling into exactly the same intuitive traps that come from failing to understand group effects. Whether they involve beer or the stock market, system-level games can serve as powerful reminders about the way we all work within complicated webs of interconnections—webs we must understand in order to thrive.

The Three Keys to Success in System Games

Among the keys to success with system games are the following:

You should do it yourself: Unlike more complicated and polished experience games, there are many software packages and resources available for creating simple system games; links to some resources are available at www.ChangingTheGameBook.com. Even more important, research has shown that putting together system models can teach you how to better manage systems yourself.[9] So not only do you get to create a training game, but you also become a better manager!

The model is the key: Start with the underlying model of the game—for example, "If players increase the number of maintenance staff in their theme park, costs go up by X amount but litter drops by Y amount." These models can usually be mocked up in a spreadsheet, and they are the heart of a system simulation. Several good introductions to modeling business dynamics are available free from MIT's System Dynamics Department Web site.

Be transparent: Unlike experience simulations, which may utilize many hidden factors (a flight simulator rarely shows you how it is calculating lift or stall speeds), system games are all about the interaction between a few key elements. Players need to have a clear idea of their roles, and the factors involved in making decisions. They will learn by interacting with the model itself and understanding how all the elements come together.

Endnotes

1. S. Weil, T.S. Hussain, T.T. Brunye, W. Ferguson, J.G. Sidman, L.L. Spahr, and B. Roberts, "Assessing the Potential of Massive Multi-Player Games to Be Tools for Military Training," The Interservice/Industry Training, Simulation & Education Conference (I/ITSEC) (2005).

2. B. Reeves and T. Malone, "Leadership in Games and at Work: Implications for the Enterprise of Massively Multiplayer Online Role-playing Games" (IBM and Seriosity, 2007).

3. A. J. Faria and W. J. Wellington, "A Survey of Simulation Game Users, Former-Users, and Never-Users," Simulation & Gaming 35.2 (2004): 178.

4. G. H. Tompson and P. Dass, "Improving Students' Self-Efficacy in Strategic Management: The Relative Impact of Cases and Simulations," Simulation & Gaming 31.1 (2000): 22.

5. J. D. Sterman, "Flight Simulators for Management Education," OR/MS Today 19.5 (1992): 40-44.

6. H. L. Lee, "Ultimate Enterprise Value Creation Using Demand-Based Management," Stanford Global Supply Chain Management Forum, Report #SGSCMF-W1-2001 (2001).

7. S. Berinato, "What Went Wrong at Cisco," CIO Magazine (2001): 10.

8. C. Thompson, "Saving the World, One Video Game at a Time," New York Times (July 23, 2006).

9. P. M. Senge, and J. D. Sterman, "Systems Thinking and Organizational Learning: Acting Locally and Thinking Globally in the Organization of the Future," in Thomas A. Kochan and Michael Useem (eds.) Transforming Organization (Oxford University Press, 1992).

CHAPTER 7

GAMES AND RECRUITING

Q uick question: What is the first ten-digit prime number contained in the mathematical constant e? We'll give you a minute to calculate it....

Did you get 7,427,466,391 as your answer? Don't worry, neither did we. This question was posed back in 2004 by a mysterious and anonymous billboard in Silicon Valley, and by a sign at a subway stop in Cambridge, Massachusetts. If you figured out the answer and went to www.7427466391.com, you were presented with another puzzle. Solve that one, and you came to a page that said, "Nice work. Well done. *Mazel tov.* You've made it to Google Labs and we're glad you're here. One thing we learned while building Google is that it's easier to find what you're looking for if it comes looking for you. What we're looking for are the best engineers in the world. And here you are."

The Google billboards are a simple but elegant illustration of the three major benefits to using games for recruiting purposes. The first benefit is that a good game will attract a large number of the right kind of candidates. Within days of the unveiling of the Google billboard, and before anyone knew Google was sponsoring it, mathematics and engineering blogs and forums were buzzing about the mysterious puzzle. No less a personality than Stephan Wolfram, the mathematical genius and entrepreneur who earned a PhD from CalTech at the age of 20, posted a solution to the puzzle in an online forum.[1] Google had obviously gotten the right pool of people interested in their game.

The second benefit is that after engaging the correct audience, recruiting games can also convey a sense of what a job will actually be like. Solving Google's puzzles involved esoteric mathematics and programming skills. The message to potential recruits was clearly that people who don't enjoy solving complex problems will probably not enjoy working at Google Labs. So merely by playing a recruiting game, players get a sense of whether they will like a job. The result is happier new hires who require less convincing than traditional job candidates.

The last and perhaps more exciting benefit of a good recruiting game is that it can filter your candidates for you. Only those people who solved the Google puzzle were invited to apply for a job through a special e-mail address. Studies show that the ability to solve difficult puzzles is a good indicator of on-the-job cognitive ability—something Google was clearly looking for. And there is an additional benefit of filtering recruits with puzzles or games—it often seems more fair and objective than other recruiting methods, and therefore leads to more satisfied candidates.[2]

All told, a recruiting game can help potential recruits find you, get them interested in your company, filter out the good prospects from the bad, and ensure that new hires know what they are in for. There are several types of recruiting games that can accomplish these goals, not just puzzle games. One approach is to use contests that encourage job candidates to compete in complex business simulations that mirror your business. Another approach is to stage recruiting events in MMOGs and virtual worlds. But perhaps the most powerful method is to create a stand-alone game that directly engages new talent, as both the army and a nonprofit research company have demonstrated.

Stand-Alone Recruiting Games

The U.S. military has the largest recruiting budget of any organization in the world. It spends upwards of $4 billion a year, including $1.6 billion on advertising alone.[3] A large percentage of this funding is spent on print and television advertising, yet a single recruiting game called *America's Army* has been, in the words of Mike Zyda, one of its creators, "the most cost-effective thing that the Army has ever done in recruiting." How effective? Advertising agency Leo Burnett conducted a survey which revealed that 30% of all Americans age 16 to 24 had a more positive impression of the Army because of the game, and, even more amazingly, the game had more impact on recruits than all other forms of Army advertising combined.[4] *America's Army* cost just $7 million to make and less than $4.5 million a year to maintain, which means that the military's most effective recruiting tool cost just .25% of the military's total advertising budget.

Figure 7.1 *America's Army* is an exciting recruiting game.
(© Army Game Project. Used with Permission.)

As one of the earliest examples of the genre, *America's Army* has become perhaps the most famous recruiting game. Distributed free on the Army's Web site, it has been among the top three most-played online games for most of this decade. It is a "first-person shooter" game, in which the player sees through the eyes, and gun sights, of his character. Most of the action takes place in a series of set-piece military scenarios: a fight to control a bridge, the ambush of a convoy, the siege of a fortified encampment. Each game involves a match, typically lasting 20 or 30 minutes, between several dozen people on two different teams, one playing defense and the other on the offense. The graphics are highly detailed, the weapons and sounds are realistic, and the action is intense—like so many other games in the genre. Except this one is available free.

But *America's Army* is designed to recruit soldiers, not just to entertain people, so there are many subtle differences between it and commercial games. For example, in a typical game, players pick sides in a conflict—Allies or Nazis, aliens or humans, Iraq or the United States—and then take on the equipment and appearance typical of their side. But in *America's Army*, it obviously wouldn't do to have some players trying to kill American soldiers, so both sides play as the United States. No matter which team they are on, when a player looks at their opponents, they see terrorists, and when they look at their teammates, they see fellow soldiers. Other design considerations include minimal violence (there is no blood to maintain a Teen rating) and stirring, patriotic briefings that precede gameplay. The result is a game tailor-made to engage a target audience—in this case, males of high-school age—and make them excited about joining the Army.

America's Army also delivers on the second goal of a recruiting game: teaching players about life in the Army. Long before players are allowed to pick up their virtual weapons and battle others online, they have to qualify as soldiers. This takes place at a virtual replica of Fort Benning in Georgia, where a virtual drill sergeant teaches players how to fire their weapons and then tests them at the rifle range. Players who fail to shoot enough targets are sent back to try again. Those who prove their skills eventually get the chance to experience advanced training, whereas those who shoot their instructor in frustration are sent to prison for a lengthy stay. Players must then complete four other realistic training scenarios based on actual Army regimens before they are able to play the combat portions of the game. And if players want to have the in-game abilities of a medic, sniper, or paratrooper, they must finish additional training courses.

Some of these training scenarios are so realistic that they almost seem like a parody. Completing the medic training, for example, requires you to sit through three PowerPoint presentations in a virtual classroom within the game. After that, you take a series of exams using a virtual pencil, with questions like "When applying a tourniquet, what information is recorded on the casualty's forehead?" In other words, it is nearly impossible to play *America's Army* without getting some sense of what it is like to actually join the Army—something the military hopes will reduce dropout rates among new recruits.

America's Army quietly accomplishes the final goal of a recruiting game by actually helping determine which players have the most potential to be soldiers. The game can track every shot fired and every movement made by its players, and it stores that information in a central database. Although *America's Army* players are not required to disclose personal information, this database enables the Army to determine a remarkable number of things about *America's Army* players, including the types of roles they like to play and their level of success in those roles, which the Army can then use to reach out to ideal recruits with in-gaming messaging, based solely on their game-playing skills. Thus, *America's Army* delivers on all three aspects of a recruiting game: engaging potential soldiers, telling them what the less objectionable parts of an Army experience might be like, and using gameplay to identify the most suitable candidates, all in one incredibly slick, if controversial, package.

While *America's Army* feels like propaganda created by the savviest of marketers, *Job of Honor* clearly represents a recruiting game devised by a Human Resources Department. Created by MITRE, a nonprofit technology think tank that serves government clients, *Job of Honor* also employs the first-person perspective of a shooter game, only this time, there is no shooting involved. Instead, you play the role of yourself, as a prospective candidate for a job at MITRE. You start in a parking lot and enter a digital version of MITRE's Massachusetts office complex. After a brief chat with the receptionist, you are taken on a tour of the campus via a golf cart driven at a very stately pace by the local HR representative, who happily extols the benefits of MITRE. Returning to campus, you go through a series of virtual interviews, and then get to experience designing an unmanned airplane. The final sequence of the game consists of flying the airplane around the MITRE complex, answering multiple-choice questions by swooping through loops that represent the possible answers.

MITRE has a very different target audience and goal than does the army. It primarily seeks out experienced engineers with masters degrees or PhDs who can qualify for security clearance. This turns out to be a relatively small group of heavily recruited people, and as MITRE's workforce has aged, securing new talent has proven to be a perpetual challenge. *Job of Honor* is MITRE's attempt to reach out to new engineers and build a lasting reputation as a cool and innovative place to work.

Figure 7.2 *Job of Honor* eschews the gunfire of America's Army for realistic virtual interviews. (Courtesy of the MITRE Corporation.)

Despite being less traditionally gamelike than *America's Army*, as well as being much cheaper and noticeably less slick, *Job of Honor* seems to work. Early college focus groups show that students who play *Job of Honor* come away significantly more likely to understand what MITRE does and what it is looking for in employees. At college career fairs, students stand in line to play the game or to watch others play, which gives MITRE's recruiters a chance to engage in longer and more detailed conversations with potential candidates than they normally would otherwise.

MITRE spent $250,000 in total to develop two different versions of *Job of Honor*. MITRE's Director of Recruiting, Gary Cluff, considers that a tremendous bargain, as $250,000 is approximately the cost of hiring just ten people through traditional recruiters. "In the long term," Cluff told us, "we think we will get many times more return on investment from this game, in terms of cost-per-hire, than we would from any other method."

Job of Honor and *America's Army* represent the ways in which custom-built, enthusiast-style games can be used for recruiting purposes. However, not all recruiting games need to be built like commercial games. Some recruiters are finding that games built around contests can be an even more effective way to reach recruits.

Recruiting Contests

L'Oréal, the French cosmetics company, is in an enviable position. Each year, more than 177,000 business students from 2,200 schools and 128 companies spend months frantically trying to demonstrate their managerial potential in the beauty products industry. They do so by managing a virtual cosmetics company in a long-running business simulation known as the *e-Strat Challenge*. Three-player teams assume the management of Prima, a cosmetics firm that is competing against computer-controlled entities called Diva, Vista, Bella, and mirror.com, in a battle over the markets for beauty cream, skin-care lotion, and other consumer products. Over the course of two real months, the *e-Strat Challenge* progresses through six rounds of six virtual months each—three years of simulated game time. Each round, players enter about 150 different choices into the simulation, ranging from R&D investments to decisions about environmentally friendly but costly manufacturing upgrades. These choices are sent back to L'Oréal, where, using real data from L'Oréal's face-cream business, the results of the players' decisions are calculated.

Each team is competing not only against their computer-controlled opponents, but also against 177,000 other players, each running his or her own version of Prima. After the first round, 1,700 teams are selected to continue, of which only 300 will proceed to the semifinals. In the end, 16 teams are invited on an all-expense-paid trip to Paris, where they participate in the final round of the competition. Finalists present a product idea in front of the top managers of L'Oréal and its consulting partners, such as McKinsey. The winning team is given a free trip anywhere in the world.

e-Strat has proven to be a terrific success for L'Oréal. It has engaged students who might not have considered a French cosmetics company as a potential employer, especially males, more technically inclined people, and students from Asia and Africa.[5] And it has offered potential new employees a chance to really experience the strategic side of the industry, helping them understand the interesting challenges that face L'Oréal as a business.

Most important, *e-Strat* is an effective talent filter. After all, the simulation is remarkably close to L'Oréal's actual business, suggesting that winners of *e-Strat* may have the motivation and talent to succeed at the real thing. And *e-Strat* creates opportunities to find new hires far from the usual recruiting grounds. Of the top teams in the 2007 round of *e-Strat*, none was from the United States, but Turkey, Indonesia, and Brazil were all represented. Even better, L'Oréal has managed to convince many of the world's top business schools to include *e-Strat* in their curricula. So it should be no surprise that the game has proven to be a good source of employees.

More than 200 people had been hired through *e-Strat* as of 2006, and another 400 have been hired through other, similar games run by L'Oréal.[6]

e-Strat is just one of many recruiting contests run by large companies, such as food giant Danone and consulting firm Booz Allen Hamilton. Danone's game, *Trust*, emphasizes corporate responsibility so successfully that it has convinced over 97% of its players that Danone is a "company that both offers good products and is a socially responsible firm."[7] Booz Allen's *CEO Challenge*, on the other hand, is an intense corporate gaming experience that accepts less than one in ten applicants from the top business schools in the country. These select few are invited to an event where they are divided into teams, each of which plays the role of a company in a highly competitive market. Over the course of a day, the teams plan, scheme, and compete to be the top dog in an evolving scenario managed by Booz Allen consultants. Although Booz Allen does not actually consider the *CEO Challenge* to be a "recruiting event," they eventually hire about 10% of its competitors.[8]

Recruiting in Virtual Worlds

Games are a powerful recruiting technique, but you do not necessarily need to create your own games to locate new talent. Virtual worlds can be ready-built locations for experiments with new recruiting techniques, as several large companies have already discovered.[9] Unsurprisingly, many of the earliest attempts at virtual world-based recruiting have occurred in *Second Life*. The largest of these efforts to date was an event sponsored by recruiting and advertising firm TMP in 2007. TMP's experiment nicely illustrates both the promise and the problems of virtual world–based recruiting.

After building an island in *Second Life*, TMP invited other companies to participate in a virtual job fair that TMP pledged to support and market. For $15,000 to $25,000 per company, TMP helped its participants construct a building on the island, which acted as a setting for interviews. The interviews themselves were to be conducted via a combination of text chat and conference calls. Most companies constructed traditional buildings, but a few forged more unique identities for themselves. Storage company EMC, for example, didn't want to blend in with a traditional brick-and-mortar building—they wanted to invoke feelings of the future. So TMP created a spherical floating office for EMC that hovered above the island. To interview with EMC, job seekers flew up a spiral stair-case, which led to individual meeting rooms.

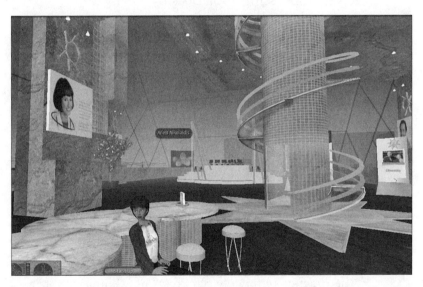

Figure 7.3   Sodexo's recruitment center in *Second Life*.
(Courtesy of Sodexo, Inc.)

Flying turned out to be more of a challenge than expected for many applicants, however. Much to the surprise of many of TMP's clients, most of the event's attendees were new to *Second Life*. One recruiter, Arie Ball of Sodexo, reported, "We thought this would be a good way to connect to Gen Y…but most of the attendees at the career fair had 5 to 15 years of job experience on average, and most of the people who came to the career fair were new to *Second Life;* they learned it to participate in the career fair." The result was some confusion as new visitors to *Second Life* had to spend hours learning the system, while other interviewees found themselves literally floating away in the middle of their interviews. Some did not even show up at all due to technical problems. In all, there were 749 individuals who requested interviews, of which 209 received them and 150 actually appeared at the right time in the right place.

Impressing Your Boss by Flying

Chef Ray Giordano wanted a job at Sodexo, the food service giant; but he lived in Las Vegas, and there were no corporate recruiters for Sodexo nearby. So Sodexo suggested that he take advantage of the company's upcoming recruiting event in *Second Life*. However, Chef Giordano was not a fan of computer games, and was more than a little nervous about the prospect of a virtual-world interview. So to prepare, he spent several hours (with the help of his children) learning how to function in *Second Life*. He created a tall, buff-looking avatar that was, according to him, "a bit different than how I look in real life." And with the help of some friendly *Second Life* residents, Chef Giordano learned how to navigate through the virtual world.

The practice ultimately paid off. Chef Giordano not only nailed his interview questions, but also taught his interviewers how to fly around and shake hands in *Second Life* (it isn't obvious how to do the latter, especially to new users of the game). Chef Giordano ended up landing the job. Although it was his resume—not his video game abilities—that ultimately made him successful, being prepared for the interview clearly made a difference. In this regard, virtual worlds are no different from the real one.

However, there certainly were a few *Second Life* natives who chose to participate in the career fair. At least a few people showed up as mermaids, Transformers, and Ewoks, but most quickly changed into more standard business attire for their actual interview. The arrival of *Second Life* regulars at a corporate event can occasionally herald disruptive activities or protests (few industry observers will forget one particular incident—an in-world CNET interview that was rather shockingly interrupted by a flock of flying genitals).[10] To reduce the risk of disruptive behavior, TMP deliberately worked with the *Second Life* community to make sure everyone felt included in the event. Russell Miyaki, the National Interactive Creative Director of TMP, noted, "There were almost no problems. We didn't want to exclude the community of *Second Life*. We wanted everyone in *Second Life* to come in, to ask questions, and to roam around. We found that it was one of the hidden codes. You want to embrace the community and involve them. We allowed anyone to have fun as long as they didn't interrupt an interview."

In the end, most of TMP's clients seem to have appreciated their *Second Life* recruiting experience, though many considered it to be more of an experiment than a major new source of employees. Companies such as Microsoft and Sodexo ultimately hired some of their interview candidates and praised the way that *Second Life* had enabled them to reach beyond their usual pool of candidates. More virtual job fairs are appearing around the world, and through them a new generation of recruiters is learning how to use virtual worlds to locate and recruit candidates. And, as games such as *Habbo Hotel* and *World of Warcraft* increasingly become places where bright, motivated individuals choose to spend their time, we expect to see recruiting in games become an increasingly important source of talent in the future. Companies that are interested in reaching people who play games, an increasingly large percentage of the workforce, will need to use games themselves to do so— whether custom-built enthusiast games or existing virtual worlds.

The Three Keys to Success in Recruiting Games

Among the keys to success with recruiting games are the following:

Know when to sell, and know when to show: A good recruiting game can be more than an advertisement for your company—it can be an opportunity to show potential employees what life in your organization is like, or an opportunity to observe and filter candidates in a whole new way. A successful recruiting game does not necessarily need to be as thorough or realistic as *America's Army*, but it also shouldn't always gloss over the negative aspects of the job for fear of repelling recruits. For example, in *Job of Honor*, players get to wander through the cube farms of MITRE. They may be less beautiful than EMC's floating sphere, but they are also potentially a better way to ensure that new hires know what they are getting into. Unrealistic advertising can leave a positive impression—and there's certainly nothing wrong with that—but realistic recruiting games can supply you with candidates who are less likely to be let down by the reality of their new jobs.

Tune in to your audience: Your goal in a recruiting game is not to make something so fun that everyone wants to play it; your goal is to make something that your target audience wants to play. Google doesn't care that 99% of people may not be familiar with the constant *e*, because their target audience is. *e-Strat* may seem too complex, but MBA students like it. Think hard about what kinds of games engage your target audience, and then build a game that suits them.

Balance engaging, teaching, and filtering: The best recruiting games accomplish three goals simultaneously: They engage your target audience, teach potential recruits about your company or your job, and filter out some candidates who don't meet your needs. This is an extremely powerful combination, but it takes balance to achieve. If a game emphasizes its filtering goals too much, it may repel an inappropriate percentage of potential recruits. If a game is too much like a real job, it may not be fun. Creating a balanced recruiting game takes time and iteration. Don't expect to create something perfect on the first, second, or even third try.

Endnotes

1. Ed Pegg and Eric Weisstein, "Mathematica's Google Aptitude," *MathWorld News* (October 13, 2004), http://mathworld.wolfram.com/news/2004-10-13/google/.

2. J. Honer, C. W. Wright, and C. J. Sablynski, "Puzzle Interviews: What Are They and What Do They Measure?" *Applied HRM Research* 11.2: 79-96.

3. "Spending on Military Recruiting," *National Priorities Project* (2007), www.nationalpriorities.org/charts/Spending-on-Military-Recruiting-2.html.

4. Shawn Zeller, "Training Games," *Government Executive* 37.1 (January 2005): 44; and Matthew Quirk, "Fun and Friendly Persuasion," *National Journal* 38.29 (July 22, 2006): 58.

5. Sharon Shinn, "Competing for Attention," *BizEd* (June 2005).

6. Ronald Alsop, "Recruiters Are Using Games to Assess MBAs," *Wall Street Journal Online* (Aug. 8, 2006), www.collegejournal.com/mbacenter/mbatrack/20060808-alsop.html?refresh=on.

7. See note 5.

8. Ronald Alsop, "M.B.A. Track: M.B.A. Recruiters Resort to Games to Spot Top Talent," *Wall Street Journal* (Aug. 8, 2006).

9. John Brown and Douglas Thomas, "You Play World of Warcraft? You're Hired!," *Wired* (Apr. 2006), www.wired.com/wired/archive/14.04/learn.html.

10. Ashlee Vance, "CNET Interviewer Assaulted by Flying Wang," *The Register* (Dec. 20, 2006), www.theregister.co.uk/2006/12/20/sadville_flyers/.

PART IV

GAMES AND THE FUTURE OF BUSINESS

Games can cause people to do amazing things, purely for the sake of fun. Consider the following four statistics: In 2007, the combined GDP of virtual worlds exceeded the GDP of several countries, including Syria, Lebanon, Latvia, and Sri Lanka.[1] In a single MMOG called *Eve Online*, players have formed 34,658 virtual companies, more than the number of food, manufacturing, textile, and office supply companies in the United States combined.[2] In less than three years, a game designed to make it fun to caption images (an important task that computers cannot easily do on their own) attracted over 22,000 players who have labeled 10 million images, with many players contributing over 40 hours a week of their time.[3] Players of *The Sims 2* have voluntarily created hundreds of thousands of freely downloadable objects for the game, including more than 20,000 kinds of chairs, almost 100,000 articles of clothing, and 52 different goatees.[4] In short, game players have been known to create vibrant economies, develop complex social systems, generate innumerable pieces of digital content, and even perform boring data entry tasks, all on an enormous scale. In some ways, gamers work harder at their games than most people do at their jobs.

There are critical lessons about the future of business to be learned from the way games inspire people and communities. For much of the past century, success was rooted in the lessons of Henry Ford: Hire employees who can do the same task repeatedly, while filling a clear role in a well-defined organization. Today, we live in a world of rapid change where innovation and quick thinking are increasingly important. Companies that rely solely on their old methods of walling themselves off from the outside world while counting on employees to voluntarily generate innovative ideas will quickly find themselves in trouble. We believe that in the future, companies that learn the lessons of games will be best able to engage the multitude of innovators and thinkers, both inside and outside their organizations, whose energy will be required to succeed in the 21st century.

The next three chapters cover the three ways in which games point the way to success in a rapidly changing business world. Chapter 8, "Games for Work, Games at Work," explores how companies can use traditional game mechanics to increase productivity. Chapter 9, "User Innovation Communities," examines how the game industry has harnessed the creative energy of its customers. Finally, Chapter 10, "Why Gamers Are Better Than Computers, Scientists, and Governments," discusses how games can be used to focus the collective knowledge of millions of people. As you'll discover, sometimes the best work can be done only through play.

Endnotes

1. Julian Dibbell, "Recalculating the Global Virtual GDP, Yet Again," *Terra Nova Blog* (June 26, 2007), http://terranova.blogs.com/terra_nova/2007/06/recalculating-t.html.

2. Eyjlfur Gumundsson, "Some Statistics on Corporations," *Economic Development Blog* (January 12, 2007), http://myeve.eve-online.com/devblog.asp?a=blog&bid=525.

3. Luis von Ahn, "Games with a Purpose," *Computer* 39.6 (June 2006): 92-94.

4. "Mod The Sims 2 Database," *Mod the Sims 2*, http://www.modthesims2.com

CHAPTER 8

GAMES FOR WORK, GAMES AT WORK

On some level, we're all familiar with the real-life importance of games and play. We know from innumerable *National Geographic* specials that cavorting lion cubs and wrestling puppies are actually preparing for serious tasks, such as attracting mates, avoiding capture, and finding food.[1] Play serves an obvious developmental role for human children as well. So many studies have demonstrated the beneficial impact of play on child development that the United Nations Commission for Human Rights has declared recreation a fundamental right of every child.[2] And as it turns out, the benefits of doing things for fun and engaging in play don't end with childhood.

Of course, we can't claim that playing *Solitaire* at work will make you smarter or better prepared (it probably won't help you attract a mate, either). But scientists have found that playing games like *Solitaire* for limited periods can potentially lead to higher morale and higher productivity.[3] Think of it as the coffee break of the new millennium. Such research into the indirect effect of games on productivity and morale, while useful, is ultimately less interesting than the growing body of research suggesting that the aspects of games that make them fun, sometimes called "game mechanics," can be used to directly increase productivity in the workplace.

In this chapter, we discuss three ways in which game mechanics can be used to make work more engaging. First, we look at what managers can learn from the way that games make time seem to fly by. Next, we examine the way that game mechanics are being used at companies like Microsoft to increase productivity. Finally, we explore some of the other ways in which games are creeping into the workplace and what that might mean for the future.

Management Lessons from Games

A question that managers don't ask enough is this: How can work be more fun, or at least more engaging? We've all experienced moments when we've felt extremely focused and productive, and time seemed to fly by. That experience was "flow," first identified by Mihaly Csikszentmihalyi in the 1970s. Flow theory describes a very focused, energized, and effective mental state that takes place when a person is fully involved in an activity.[4] Flow, also colloquially known as "being in the zone," is most stereotypically reported by famous sports figures after winning a particularly intense game, but it can be common at work as well. Experiencing flow at work has been linked to increased performance and improved learning,[5] as well as increased productivity and problem solving.[6] As it turns out, several of the factors that contribute to flow also underlie good game design, most particularly factors related to goals, feedback, and difficulty.

The activities most likely to result in a state of flow are those that have clear goals and provide quick, unambiguous feedback. Without these, people cannot know what needs to be done in any given situation and therefore will be of limited effectiveness. Fortunately, games excel in expressing this sort of information. Whether they are gobbling dots in *Pac-Man* or slaying monsters in *World of Warcraft*, players know exactly what they should be doing ("eat dots, avoid ghosts"), the consequences of failure ("the ghost eats you—lose one life"), and the benefits of success ("high score!"). Compare this to so many work situations that are plagued with fuzzy goals ("satisfy our customers") and slow feedback loops ("you aren't being promoted because you failed to satisfy customers for the past six months"). Businesses can learn much from games simply by trying harder to clarify employee goals and improve feedback loops. The goal to "satisfy customers" becomes "satisfy at least 20 customers a day," and biannual career checkpoints are augmented with real-time customer feedback fed directly to employees.

Activities that lead to flow also need to have the right level of difficulty. Our lives are rarely balanced to the extent that we might like. We are, at any given moment, too busy or bored, overwhelmed or underchallenged, exhausted or restless. Good games, on the other hand, excel at consistently confronting players with structured and novel challenges that are neither too easy nor too difficult. The ghosts in *Pac-Man* become a little bit faster with each stage cleared; higher-level monsters in *World of Warcraft* have unique abilities and are harder to kill. This is one reason why flow is so common in the context of games, and so uncommon in the business world. Businesses that can do more to dynamically adjust the challenges facing their employees, in tune with their evolving abilities, will be rewarded with higher morale and greater productivity. For example, a high-performing employee might be recognized with a promotion and also have her goal shifted from "satisfy at least 20 customers a day" to "satisfy at least 20 customers and resolve at least 5 customer escalations."

Making work more gamelike through clearer goals, quicker feedback, and more finely tuned challenges has the potential to be extremely effective. However, we must caution that it also has the potential to go terribly wrong. Tinkering with goals, in particular, can be a very tricky thing. In the sales world, the wrong goal can quickly result in a wave of quickly negotiated contracts that your business can't actually fulfill. A customer support representative with the goal of "satisfying at least 20 customers a day" might do so by making costly concessions to customers who merely required verbal support. These issues can be addressed through more nuanced goals, but making a goal both nuanced and clear isn't easy. As such, we recommend that companies who want to build game-like principles into their core business first carefully test the impact of doing so, preferably on sub-units of larger teams.

Fortunately, there are less-risky ways to integrate productivity-boosting game mechanics into your business. These methods generally involve two things: friendly competition, and the use of status symbols like high scores, virtual badges of achievement, and "rare" virtual items.

Using Games to Motivate Productivity

In Chapter 1, "An Introduction to Games, and Why They Matter," we mentioned that players of *World of Warcraft* and other MMOGs have been known to spend countless hours engaging in a tedious practice that the gamer community has labeled "grinding." Grinding takes many forms, all of which are startlingly similar to rote work. For example, a player might grind (i.e., kill) the same monster over and over again, for tens of hours, in hopes of winning a rare virtual item that appears only once in every hundred kills on average. Grinding is also a characteristic of many tasks that a player might perform as part of a virtual profession that they role-play in games. *World of Warcraft* has several professions, including leatherworking and blacksmithing, each of which requires long hours of repetitive work by players who want to improve their skills and craft the best virtual items their virtual trade has to offer.

So during a bad day at the office, you may want to consider how your job compares to that of a chef, one of the easier professions in *World of Warcraft*. To advance to the highest level as a chef, a player must make 60 loaves of bread, 80 spiced wolf-meat snacks,

70 crab cakes, 50 "curiously tasty omelets" (made with dinosaur eggs), 100 wolf ribs, 100 wolf steaks, 75 fillets of dangerous fish, and a whole lot of crunchy serpent. Now consider that prospective master-chefs must actually hunt those serpents, raptors, and wolves before cooking them—a very time-intensive process! Most cooks in real life don't need to kill their own entrees, and none pays $15 per month for the privilege of clocking in to work.

Similarly, many players of Xbox 360 games are committed to increasing their gamerscore and earning achievements—two measures of status that have become a core part of the Xbox experience. Every Xbox 360 game awards a certain number of gamerscore points and achievements (which are basically like merit badges) whenever players complete a predefined challenge, such as "hit a grand slam" in a baseball game, or "win first place three times in a row" in a racing game. Most of these achievements are genuinely fun to earn as part of the normal process of playing a game, but there are certainly a few that are simply a time-consuming pain. Nevertheless, many players will do whatever it takes to win every achievement in a game, even when they have already tired of playing the game. You might assume that this sort of reward-chasing is limited to the young, but that is not the case. Pogo.com, a casual game portal that caters to adults, has its own form of achievements called "badges." Like achievements, badges are awarded for completing tasks like "win eight *Solitaire* games in the next 24 hours." And, like achievements, badges have proven to be incredibly powerful drivers of consumer behavior, even for 50-year-old men and women.

The Xbox 360 Live system also features leaderboards, which are basically lists of high scores associated with each Xbox 360 game. Leaderboards, like achievements and gamerscore, are an incentive for people to play games. When they perform well enough, players will reach the top of a weekly or even all-time leaderboard, which is visible to all their friends. Leaderboard scores, achievements, badges, and gamerscore have zero monetary value, and they also cannot be traded, which eliminates any possibility of their use as a virtual currency. And though achievements are occasionally used by game developers to reinvent parts of their game (for example, the "Pacifist" achievement in a game called *Geometry Wars* requires players to *not* fire their guns for 60 seconds, a voluntary act that completely changes the gameplay experience), most achievements are simply more of a status symbol.

Why are video game players willing to spend so much time and effort earning virtual items and status symbols like achievements? We admit that this is a complicated question with no simple answer. Virtual items, in particular, are often not only status symbols in MMOGs but also much-needed tools without which players cannot succeed in the game. Nevertheless, it is fair to say that one very important factor driving the interest in leaderboards, achievements, and virtual items boils down to status and friendly competition. People want to feel good about themselves, and these mechanisms are a convenient source of gratification. People also tend to especially enjoy competition when the consequences of losing are relatively trivial. Games with weekly leaderboards provide ample opportunity for friends to compete with each other in a fun, highly repeatable, and low-stakes manner.

Although many businesses have attempted to harness elementary competitive elements in order to improve morale and productivity ("the first sales team to move 100 units wins a prize!"), few have leveraged leaderboards to the extent that games do, and almost none have experimented with achievements and virtual item–based rewards. However, we have begun to see tantalizing hints of the potential for these mechanisms in business environments. One of the best examples can be found within the walls of Microsoft—but not within its Xbox division. As it turns out, the engineers behind Windows Vista are far ahead of Microsoft's own game gurus when it comes to play and corporate productivity.

Necessity is the mother of invention, and the Vista development team certainly had its fair share of need. As the next version of Windows, Vista was guaranteed to hit the desktops of millions of people in a fairly short period postlaunch. For obvious reasons, the Vista team needed to catch as many bugs as possible before the software was released. One of the most practical ways to do this was to rope as many Microsoft employees as possible into helping test Vista on their own PCs. Ross Smith, Microsoft's Director of Test for the Windows Defect Prevention Team, knew that the typical volunteer recruiting process just wasn't going to cut it. He explained, "Typically, any project cycle starts out with the team that needs help sending out a mail asking for help. Five people sign up. So the team asks a manager for help, and he sends out a mail, and ten more people sign up. This goes on and on, until the team reaches out to a Senior VP, and he sends out a mail to his entire division. Then 100 more people sign up. It's understandable; people are busy doing their own jobs and this stuff can be a hassle."

So, with the help of several different groups across the Vista organization, the Windows Defect Prevention team set out to change the bug testing paradigm at Microsoft. They created an extremely simple game called *The Beta1 Game*. To play, all you needed to do was install an early "beta" version of the Vista software. Doing this would earn you a *b*. Voting on the version would earn you an *e*, and running your version overnight would earn you a *t*, and so forth. Everyone who participated in the game could see the letters earned by everyone else who participated. And that's all there was to it.

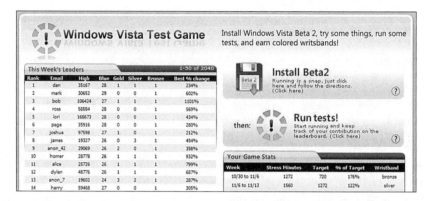

Figure 8.1 Using leaderboards and encouraging friendly competition through *The Beta2 Game* helped Microsoft quadruple participation in an otherwise boring task. (Reprinted with permission from Microsoft)

Beta1 certainly doesn't sound like much, but according to Smith and his colleague, Robert Musson, it quadrupled participation in typically troublesome facets of the Vista testing effort. Smith, who has since become a dedicated proponent of games in the workplace, notes, "We didn't do anything special to promote *Beta1*. We sent the same e-mail we always do. But because there was a game and there was competition, participation skyrocketed. People were talking smack in the halls and bragging about their status on the leaderboards. VPs would run into my office and yell, 'Where's my *e*? I earned it last night!'"

The Windows Defect Prevention team was so encouraged by the success of *Beta1* that it followed up immediately with *The Beta2 Game*. *Beta2* expanded on the original concept by awarding points for a wider variety of activities, instead of five fixed characters. Like *Beta1*, it had leaderboards, but it also had prizes and random drawings. Players could also earn wristbands, which served as physical representations of their success in the game. Once again, participation in the test regime quadrupled.

By all accounts, *Beta1* and *Beta2* were a remarkable success. As games go, they may have been quite simplistic, but they cost almost nothing to develop and accomplished their objective. Smith and Musson believe that with a bit more time and expense, they could have developed games that were even more effective. They did not, for example, have an achievement system to go along with the leaderboards, which might have helped focus players' energy even more effectively. Or imagine if all Microsoft employees had avatars that were prominently featured within the corporate intranet. What might have happened if *Beta1* and *Beta2* players could win virtual items for these avatars, especially rare items awarded with low probability, as is the case with MMOGs like *World of Warcraft*?

Avatar-based productivity games may seem like a giant leap, but such games are already finding their way into consumers' homes. *Handipoints*, a virtual world launched in November 2007, enables parents to award virtual currency, as well as real-world rewards like physical toys, to children for completing chores, brushing their teeth, and eating healthy food. Kids spend their points on virtual items for their avatar, or to watch cartoons and play minigames within the virtual world. In five months, *Handipoints* has attracted 150,000 users, about one-third of whom are parents while the remaining two-thirds are children.[7]

Handipoints is not the only start-up hoping to use virtual currency to improve productivity. Seriosity, IBM's research partner in the MMOG leadership study we cited earlier, has developed a system called *Attent*, which basically boils down to a virtual currency, the "Serio," that can be attached to corporate e-mail. The more important you believe your message to be, the more Serios you attach to it in hopes that recipients will take the message seriously. Seriosity, which is still privately testing *Attent* with initial partners, claims that users of Serios have already demonstrated improved response times when replying to important e-mails. And although *Attent*'s potential effectiveness seems somewhat limited in the absence of other virtual-world elements that lend meaning to virtual currency, it is not hard to imagine how *Attent,* and other corporate systems like it, might someday evolve to more closely resemble *Habbo Hotel* and *Handipoints* than anything currently on the market.

Making Work Look Like a Game

Which would you rather stare at all day?

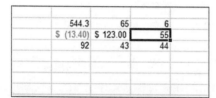

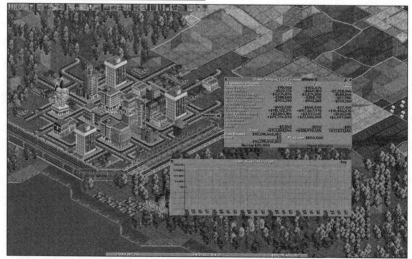

Figure 8.2 Two very different interfaces for similar data. (Game image from *OpenTTD*)

This is increasingly more than just a hypothetical question. Computer games such as *SimCity* intuitively enable middle schoolers to manage dozens of variables, ranging from crime to pollution. Virtual worlds like *Second Life* offer more interesting environments for meetings than teleconferences or even actual conference rooms.

The user interface of *The Sims* has been tested and refined far more than most office productivity applications. So it is perhaps not surprising that the look and feel of games is increasingly finding its way into the workplace.

One of the pioneers of this movement is a program called *PSDoom*, which is based on a popular shooter game released in the early 1990s. In *Doom*, you play the role of a space marine fighting the forces of Hell in an abandoned base on Mars. The game is played from the first-person perspective; that is, you see the game environment through the eyes of your character, which increases the feeling of immersion in the game. The plotline of *Doom* may not have been much to be proud of, but the game featured great graphics, exciting gameplay, and more than a few thrilling moments that made you want to play with the lights on. Dennis Chao, a graduate student at the University of New Mexico, realized that IT system administrators coincidentally shared a common vocabulary with *Doom* players, included "killing" errant programs, encountering computer processes called "daemons," and "fighting for resources." So Dennis built *PSDoom*, which used the *Doom* game as an interface for IT system administration.

Instead of working with lines of text, *PSDoom* represents each program running in a computer's memory as a monster in the game, making it easy to tell when a computer is running too many programs simultaneously. Shooting a monster reduces the amount of computer processing power dedicated to the program it represents; killing a monster terminates the related program.[8] The *PSDoom* project, which was never publicized by Chao, nevertheless attracted tens of thousands of visitors per day within a week of being revealed on Chao's Web site. While primarily an experiment, *PSDoom* showed that games can be a more intuitive way to display complex information, and that public interest in such solutions is strong.

Visitorville, a traffic-monitoring application for Web sites, is another tool that uses gamelike interfaces to make data easier to understand and process. *Visitorville* turns your Web site into a virtual city. Little people, representing your Web site's visitors, arrive into town via labeled buses (i.e., search engines) and wander among buildings that represent the individual pages of your Web site. The result is a much more intuitive way of observing traffic flow. In the future, we expect more of the business world to incorporate the lessons of *PSDoom* and *Visitorville* in making work look more like a game.

This is already occurring through the increasing use of virtual worlds for teleconference meetings. NASA, IBM, and Cisco have all begun experimenting with meetings in virtual worlds such as *Second Life*. These virtual worlds also enable geographically dispersed individuals to share and work together on virtual prototypes. For example, one coalition of forward-thinking architects has begun using *Second Life* as a collaborative design space, within which they have already designed a health facility for an organization that provides medical services to rural residents of western Nepal.[9] These architects have dubbed the tools and processes they use in *Second Life* "wikitecture," a play on the name of the technology that drives collaborative knowledge systems such as Wikipedia.[10] Like users of Wikipedia, these wikitecture users iterate on one another's work, greatly polishing it over time. Their efforts are just one example of how virtual worlds are becoming useful spaces for meetings and collaborative activities.

The Four Keys to Success When Making Work Feel More Like Play

Among the keys to success for making work feel like play are the following:

Be careful when assigning a score to anything: As we've noted earlier, people are very good at finding holes in game logic and developing ways to "cheat" the system. Given this, you must not tie game-based achievements, such as reaching the top of a monthly leaderboard, to highly significant real-world rewards, such as bonuses or promotions. Not only would doing so encourage rampant cheating, but it might also open the proverbial Pandora's box and encourage harmful activities that do not actually maximize business value. It might also turn employees against one another. Games in the workplace are most effective when players want to win because winning is fun, not because losing hurts. When a big monetary bonus is on the line, a friendly game can become something else.

When you're assigning a score to any business activity, we recommend that you first run a small test using a pilot group. Even a small number of players will prove themselves remarkably adept at finding loopholes in your system. With time and iteration, you can develop a system that not only encourages a certain behavior (that is, "find bugs in Windows Vista") but encourages the *most useful* behavior (that is, "find high-priority bugs that cause Vista to crash").

Status symbols are most potent when used consistently across an organization: Game-based achievements are more effective when more people are familiar with them. Imagine how useless Boy Scout merit badges would be if only ten people on Earth knew what they were. The situation wouldn't be any better if Boy Scouts used 20 separate, distinct badge systems for measuring achievement. If you're going to build a variety of productivity games into your business, make sure that a large pool of people—for example, an entire division, at very least—all use the same achievement, virtual item, and/or currency system. With each new game you integrate into the system, your platform will become more influential and more entertaining.

Don't turn your employees into "losers": One of the great things about many video games is that they don't split players into winners and losers. Users of Pogo.com are competing against themselves, not against other players when they tackle challenges in hopes of winning a badge. Two people, one with 50 badges and one with 100 badges, are "a winner and a bigger winner," not "a loser and a winner." Productivity games should be designed, in general, to elicit the same sense of shared progress or, at most, very friendly competition.

Keep it simple: Productivity games do not need to match the complexity of a typical *Dungeons & Dragons* role-playing game. They should be simple, engaging experiences that work for the vast majority of your employees. Simple games also have the benefit of being relatively easier to launch and easier to administer.

Endnotes

1. Robin Marantz Henig, "Taking Play Seriously," *New York Times* (February 17, 2008), www.nytimes.com/2008/02/17/magazine/17play.html.

2. United Nations, "Convention on the Rights of the Child," (1989) UN, New York.

3. "Games at Work May Be Good for You," *BBC Online* (November 7, 2003), http://news.bbc.co.uk/2/hi/technology/3247595.stm.

4. Mihaly Csikszentmihalyi and Isabella Selega, *Optimal Experience: Psychological Studies of Flow in Consciousness* (Cambridge University Press, 1988).

5. R. W. Quinn "Flow in Knowledge Work: High Performance Experience in the Design of National Security Technology," *Administrative Science Quarterly* 50.4 (2005).

6. Charalampos Mainemelis, "When the Muse Takes It All: A Model for the Experience of Timelessness in Organizations," *Academy of Management Review*, 26.4 (Oct. 2001).

7. Mark Hendrickson, "Handipoints Thinks a Virtual World Could Make Kids Do Chores in the Real One," *Techcrunchm* (March 27, 2008), www.techcrunch.com/2008/03/27/handipoints-thinks-a-virtual-world-could-make-kids-better-in-the-real-one/.

8. D. L. Chao, "Computer games as interfaces," *interactions*, 11.5 (2004): 71-72.

9. "Nepal Challenge 2007," AMD Open Architecture Network, www.openarchitecturenetwork.org/challenge/asia.

10. Ryan Schultz and Jon Brouchoud, "The Final Design: Wikitecture 3.0," *Studio Wikitecture* (March 4, 2008), http://studiowikitecture.wordpress.com/2008/03/04/the-final-design-wikitecture-30-thank-you/.

CHAPTER 9

USER INNOVATION COMMUNITIES

If games can inspire employees to be more productive, it should be no surprise that game players might also be willing to invest countless hours in improving the games that they are fans of. For example, in the two years following its release, over $16.5 million worth of labor was invested in the popular World War II game *Battlefield 1942*.[1] This work, which greatly enhanced the game, was performed entirely by fans, for free. Working individually or in teams, these fans voluntarily created a wide variety of mods (modifications) for *Battlefield 1942*, some of which represented over 1,000 hours of work.

The content created by players of *Battlefield 1942* did not appear by accident, or without encouragement. Game companies have spent many years learning how to channel the passion of their user communities into mutually beneficial work. These lessons are increasingly important to every industry, because games are not the only products that attract communities of user innovators. Extreme sports nuts, granola-bar enthusiasts, fans of LEGO toys, lovers of TiVo digital video recorders, and Toyota Prius drivers, among hundreds more, have formed documented online social groups where users actively help one another modify the products they are passionate about. In fact, it is extremely rare to find industries that *don't* attract user innovation communities. (As an interesting experiment, you might want to search the Internet for forums, wikis, and mailing lists that focus on your products. What you find might surprise you.)

This not a new phenomenon; customers have been modifying and improving products since long before the days of video games, though not always to the delight of the makers of those products. For example, in the 1960s and 1970s, there was a large community of bright geeks who turned their substantial intellects to less corporate-friendly forms of innovation. Known as "phone phreaks," these individuals spent their time learning how to manipulate the AT&T long-distance network and building devices that could be used to trick the system into giving out free calls. Ironically, many years later, two of those phone phreaks would end up being responsible for a resurgence of AT&T. Those enterprising hackers were Steve Jobs and Steve Wozniak, the future founders of Apple, whose iPhone has boosted a much-diminished AT&T to new heights.[2] Both the phone phreaks covertly exploring the inner workings of AT&T and the friendly modders improving *Battlefield 1942* illustrate an increasingly important phenomenon: user innovation communities.

Though many companies don't recognize it, user innovation turns out to be one of the most important sources of breakthrough innovations. In research conducted at MIT, Professor Eric von Hippel discovered that between 10% and 40% of the users of products ranging from surgical devices to sports equipment have modified these items to better fit their needs.[3] This sort of user innovation occurs whenever manufactured solutions do not exactly match the needs of users—whether it be a college kid who wants to play a version of *Battlefield 1942* set in the *Star Wars* universe, an auto enthusiast who wants his car to accelerate faster, or a world-class surgeon who finds that existing medical devices can't support her latest innovative procedure. In all of these cases, users have understood their own problems and desires better than corporations, and have sought to satisfy their needs on their own. The college kid creates the *Star Wars Battlefield* mod; the auto enthusiast modifies the computer chip in his car's engine; and the surgeon invents a new type of cardiac catheter.

As Professor von Hippel has demonstrated, it is often users—not manufacturers—who are responsible for breakthrough innovation, though manufacturers often benefit both directly and indirectly from users' efforts. Roughly 80% of breakthrough innovation in scientific instruments, 70% of breakthrough innovation in semiconductor processes, and 60% of breakthrough innovation in sports equipment can ultimately be traced back to users.[4] Successfully managing user innovators, and the communities of which they are a part, is increasingly proving to be a key to success for companies in competitive fields.

So what does all this have to do with games? More than any other industry, video game companies have succeeded in harnessing the positive aspects of user innovation. They understand the promise and the peril of user innovation communities and have developed powerful methods of managing them. This chapter delves into some of these techniques, and is a bit different from the rest of the book as a result. Rather than focusing on what games can do for your company, this chapter explores the lessons we can learn from game companies themselves, and the ways they encourage users to do free work for them.

The Motivations of User Innovators

Positive relationships with innovative user communities begin with the realization that there is no "natural" connection between the goals of users and the goals of companies. Companies want to make a profit, but user innovators want to solve their own problems, gain status within their communities, or just have fun. This explains the awkward dynamic that has developed between a company like Sony, which released its PlayStation Portable (PSP) gaming device with safeguards that prevent the PSP from running programs not approved by Sony, and the PSP user community. After all, Sony expected to profit by charging consumers for new games, movies, and other content, especially since they were probably taking a loss on the sale of the device itself.[5] But some of the brightest users of the PSP didn't care about Sony's business plan—they wanted to use the cutting-edge device for other purposes, such as surfing the Web, viewing a wide variety of movies, playing homemade games, or, more alarmingly, pirating commercial games.

Within days of the release of the PSP, clever users had discovered how to modify the PSP's software with a "home-brew" version that enabled them to do whatever they wanted with the PSP, much to Sony's dismay. And, despite years of trying to relock the PSP through software updates, a large community of active user innovators continues to counter Sony's every move. The result, in Sony's view, is a damaged business—one in which sales of low-margin PSPs are pushed higher by consumers who will then use the devices to consume content from which Sony does not profit.[6]

It is easy to blame the undermining of the PSP business plan on irresponsible hackers, as Sony did, with a dire warning implying that any modification was a "form of piracy" and cautioning that "any hacking or homebrew applications may cause damage to the PSP unit, and will void the warranty."[7] But this is, at best, willful ignorance of the goals of many in the PSP home-brew community. For example, would purely malicious hackers spend thousands of hours creating software that enables the PSP to edit documents, read comic books, perform math calculations, and even teach basic Greek and Japanese? And PSP user innovators have also created hundreds of original games for the platform, all available for free to those who are willing to modify their PSP to accept non-Sony software. Of course, a major driver behind the popularity of home-brew PSP software is the fact that it enables consumers to play pirated games, but that is far from the only goal of this sophisticated and complex community.

Hacking with Haikus

One of the more interesting examples of how a user innovation community responded to industry attempts to shut it down occurred in January of 2000. At issue were a few pages of software code, known as DeCSS, which allowed anyone with a computer to be able to play DVDs, something previously limited to certain types of computer operating systems. A side effect of DeCSS was that it would allow DVDs to be copied, so the movie industry worked hard to prevent the software from spreading. The movie industry's lawyers received an injunction in January of 2000 to prevent anyone from displaying or linking to the source code of the software, an act considered by many programmers to be a violation of free speech.

The software development community reacted almost immediately, but not in the way the movie industry wanted. It became fashionable to come up with as many ways to share the DeCSS code as possible. Hackers began printing the DeCSS source on T-shirts (later the subject of another lawsuit), writing rock songs using the code, hiding it in images, and even creating an epic 456-stanza haiku, which described the exact process needed to decode a DVD. More ominously for the movie industry, community members began to compete against each other to generate the smallest, most elegant piece of software possible that could be used to copy DVDs, eventually shrinking the process to seven simple lines of code. Far from preventing the spread of DeCSS, the actions of the movie industry only increased its visibility.

Most companies, when confronted by innovative user communities, see only the downside and use every legal means at their disposal to attack the communities. This usually radicalizes the community against the company. User communities often feel that they are doing a company a favor by improving its products, but when the legal gloves come off, an all-out war is usually the result. For example, the early phone phreakers often had high opinions of AT&T, and many wanted to work for the company someday. They viewed their exploration of the phone system as a technical challenge, not a form of theft.[8] But once AT&T noticed that its system was being manipulated, it went after phreakers in a big way, getting laws passed in many states that made phreaking illegal, and enabling AT&T to go on a witch hunt. Between 1965 and 1970, about 30 million calls were searched without notice by the company, and 1.5 million calls were recorded, resulting in the capture of 500 phreakers. In return, the phreakers became motivated not only to explore the phone system, but to undermine it. The result was a war that cost both sides dearly and resulted in a decade-long stalemate. The same pattern has been repeated in many other industries since then. Fortunately, there is a better way to balance the risks and rewards of user innovation communities—a way pioneered by video game companies.

What Game Companies Know about User Communities

Game companies are not immune to both the positive and the negative aspects of user innovation. Game mods may increase the value of a game, but they may also detract from the sales of official expansion packs. Encouraging people to modify a game can also make it easier for them to get around copy protections and illegally copy the program. (This was especially true in the early days of computer games, when elaborate copy protection systems were built into the software.) Building active communities around games, and especially MMOGs, can increase consumer loyalty, but it also creates an echo chamber in which criticisms of a game or its developer can spiral out of control. With these potential pitfalls in mind, game companies throughout the 1980s and early 1990s did what so many companies do today: They kept their systems closed and proprietary, and did their best to discourage people from altering or modifying their games.

This all changed in 1993, when id Software released *Doom*, the first-person shooter game. *Doom* took off after being released on the still-new Internet, reaching millions of computers. One of the defining features of *Doom* was that, despite the misgivings of some id Software executives, it was one of the first games to embrace user innovators, allowing people to create their own content.[9] This change of heart was encouraged by the lead programmer of *Doom*, John Carmack, who felt that "information should be free."[10] But the success of their experiment impressed even Carmack. More than 12,000 modifications were released for *Doom*, a remarkable number in the days before the World Wide Web. Notably, most of these mods complied with the request of Doom's makers: that user modifications work only on copies of *Doom* that had been legally purchased. By engaging directly with the user community, id Software not only benefited from user innovation, but also protected itself to some extent from the dark side of user communities.

After *Doom* became a hit, many game companies realized that they could generate potentially huge returns by embracing innovative users. Some of these efforts were remarkably successful. The *Counter-Strike* mod turned a popular science fiction "shooter" game, *Half-Life*, into a team-based game featuring terrorists and counter-terrorists. *Counter-Strike* became a massive hit in its own right, encouraging many consumers who may not have been interested in *Half-Life* to buy it anyway, just so they could play the modified version. Valve soon hired the team of users who created *Counter-Strike*, and a subsequent commercial release of the game went on to sell more than two million copies. It was, for many years, the most played PC game online.

There are two general lessons that can be learned from how game companies manage their user innovation communities. First, game companies align the needs of user communities with their own needs by offering awards and incentives that make it fun and interesting to focus on business-positive innovation, while discouraging detrimental activity such as piracy. id Software's relationship with its user community is an excellent example. Second, game companies provide their customers tools and support that make it easier for them to innovate in a positive way, while making unwanted innovation more of a hassle. Both aspects are critical to managing innovative user communities.

Aligning Communities

People in the game industry have long discovered that user communities will form spontaneously around their games, like it or not. And almost as inevitably, those communities will begin to create, modify, and share game content. Some of these innovations, such as mods like *Counter-Strike*, will be positive, whereas others, such as ways to circumvent copy protection, will not. How can companies steer user communities toward the good stuff and away from the bad? Game developers have answered this question, in part, simply by realizing that innovative user communities are an increasingly important part of their business—one that merits a specialized "community manager" to oversee. Community managers inherit a wide variety of functions that cut across marketing, PR, and even technical support, and focus entirely on relating to and working with the user community.

Good community managers understand that, in the words of one professional, "A gaming community is like a country, with its own language, [and] its own culture and rules." [11] A good game company takes the time to learn the language and rules of that community, and only then can it start carefully guiding the community toward productive, rather than destructive, user innovation. The goal is to create a mutually beneficial situation in which both the community and the company are happy. There are two main ways to achieve this:

Recognize your users: Lars Bo Jeppesen and Lars Frederiksen, two business school professors who study innovation, wanted to understand why user innovators almost always freely give away their work. Wouldn't it make more sense, at least in some cases, to try selling or licensing their innovations? In a detailed study of user innovators in the electronic musical instrument space, they found an answer to their question. It turns out that users are highly motivated by feedback and praise from the company that created the product which serves as the basis for their innovation.[12] The desire to be recognized by the company is, in many cases, a powerful enough incentive that it encourages many users to give away their innovations for free, simply in hopes of receiving praise.

Game developers, which tend to attract very enthusiastic fans, have come to intuitively understand the importance of customer recognition, and have developed a wide range of methods via which to recognize user innovators. Individual players might be given virtual badges of achievement, like those mentioned in the preceding chapter. Fan-created Web sites might be given exclusive access to information about upcoming game releases. High-quality user-created content might be acknowledged by the company on an official Web site or in an official blog posting. Truly excellent content might even be incorporated into a future version of the game.

Some game companies have even made a point of hiring the most talented user innovators. This is perhaps the most wonderful and simultaneously self-serving form of user recognition, because great talent is extremely hard to find! Savvy game companies have even launched modding competitions, for which the grand prize includes—you guessed it—a job working for the company. Such competitions are extremely cost-effective, and can generate tremendous excitement and customer loyalty.

User innovators are also motivated by the recognition of their fellow community members, not just recognition from the company. There are a number of causes for this, including the desire to be liked, the expectation that helping the community entitles you to be helped in the future, and the hope that community connections might lead to a job or other opportunities someday.[13] Businesses can help by providing formal mechanisms through which users can rate each other's contributions to the community. One example of a nongame business that has done this is Threadless, an online T-shirt company whose revenues rose from $600,000 in 2003 to approximately $30 million in 2007. Threadless has not designed a single one of its products—instead, a community of 400,000 people do all the design work for the company. Each day, at least 150 users submit designs for T-shirts, which the community votes on. Threadless then sells the ten best-liked designs each week.

Work directly with the community and its leaders: The social systems of a user community tend to evolve on their own; however, companies can still work with a community and its leaders to prevent the culture of the community from veering to the counterproductive, as happened with AT&T and the phreakers. Many game companies have helped shape user communities by reaching out to influential community members, educating them on matters of importance to the company, and listening to their grievances. In an increasing number of cases, game companies have helped formally establish semiofficial user communities around their products, and have helped those communities define rules that promote positive behavior.

However, many user communities are often quite sensitive to being "handled," and can quickly lose faith in a company that seems to be manipulating them. One famous case of community manipulation even led to the equivalent of a political revolution. The space-themed MMOG *Eve Online* features huge teams of players who engage in continuous, epic battles over virtual star systems. In 2006, the *Eve Online* player community discovered that one particularly powerful team was being given special help by an employee of CCP, the developer of the game. Though the immediate scandal was quickly resolved, a whiff of corruption lingered over *Eve Online*, alienating many of its players. In a unique move, CCP responded by establishing the Council of Stellar Management, a democratically elected group of players who would oversee *Eve Online*. CCP even offered to regularly fly members of the Council to Iceland, where CCP is based, so that they can audit CCP's operations and report back to the player community. CCP also called in election monitors from universities in Europe and the United States, in hopes of legit-imizing the newly created Council and avoiding further scandal.[14] As Eve Online clearly demonstrates, recovering from community mis-management can be costly, so honesty and openness are crucial to a healthy relationship with any user community.

Equipping Communities

Merely aligning the goals of communities with the goals of compa-nies is not quite enough to take full advantage of the power of user innovation. After all, once you have a community in sync with your company, you want to empower it to do amazing things so that as many of your users as possible are innovating, sharing ideas, and refining each other's concepts. Fortunately, there are at least two well-developed ways to encourage user innovation and channel it down useful paths:

Give your users content-creation toolkits: Why should user innovation be hard? Many game companies have created spe-cial toolkits that allow nontechnical customers to make mods and create game content without learning a programming language, by using a simple graphic interface. In some cases, users even improve on the toolkits themselves. *Second Life, Neverwinter Nights,* and *The Sims* are all examples of games previously mentioned that have very successfully leveraged simple toolkits to encourage user innovation.

Good toolkits are fun, powerful, and easy to use, and often require as much effort to develop as a game itself. Fortunately, the effort is well worth it. A good toolkit not only encourages innovation, but also makes customers feel much more strongly about a product. One study using toolkits for watch design found that consumers would be willing to pay 100% more if they had helped design the product through a toolkit.[15] User innovation tools have also been shown to help predict which future products might succeed; for example, if players keep using the tools to add realistic cars to *The Sims*, an automobile-themed expansion pack might be a very good idea.[16]

Toolkits have found success far beyond the world of games. For example, in the late 1990s, GE Plastics spent about $5 million to create an online toolkit that enabled users to virtually experiment with polymers sold by the company. By 2002, the toolkit had attracted a million visitors per year, who accounted for one-third of all new customer leads. And because the toolkit enabled people to experiment in a manner that would previously have required real products (and greater expense), GE Plastics' customer service call volume was cut in half.[17]

Encourage your users to assist one another: Another way that companies can channel the efforts of users into particularly valuable areas is by enabling user-to-user assistance. User-to-user assistance, which often takes place in online message boards and forums, can take the form of mundane technical support ("Why does the game keep shutting down?") or expert assistance ("I want to mod the game so that it includes *Star Wars* characters; how do I do that?"). The monetary value of user-to-user technical support alone is impressive. One study of the game *Red Alert* found that user-to-user support substituted for the equivalent of three full-time employees, each working for 45 hours a week, and suggested that this might be typical for the game industry.[18]

In general, large user communities are remarkably efficient at providing support to community members, mainly because large communities are very diverse. Studies that have looked at user-to-user support in industries other than the game industry have found that most people's questions are answered quickly and easily, because there is always someone in the community to whom the answer was already known. In fact, it often takes just two minutes or less of a community expert's time to answer a typical question.[19] A large number of nongame companies also encourage user-to-user assistance, including Microsoft. By leveraging recognition and nonmonetary awards, Microsoft's MVP program has encouraged thousands of highly skilled professionals to assist other users for free.

Toolkits and user-to-user assistance are just two ways of getting user communities to work for you. Any user community that is aligned with the goals of your company will be a powerful source of innovation and new products. Though the examples in this chapter are drawn from the game industry, a huge body of academic work shows that user communities exist almost everywhere. Increasingly, researchers who study innovation believe that it is the companies that best harness the power of user innovation that will succeed in a rapidly changing world.[20]

The Four Keys to Working with User Innovation Communities

Among the keys to working with user innovation communities are the following:

You can't stop communities, but you can guide them: User innovation communities will appear around your product whether you like it or not. If you do not provide a place for these communities to reside, such as by hosting discussion forums on your company's Web site, they will find another site from which to operate. And no matter where the community resides, it won't automatically share the same goals as your company, so you need to work with the community. You can choose to ignore user communities, but you usually shouldn't.

Don't try to manipulate communities: Transparent attempts to manipulate user communities almost always fail, and fail spectacularly, as they did in *Eve Online*. Holding back information from user communities might be okay, but deception is usually discovered and punished. The best way to deal with user communities is to be honest with them.

Communities can be aligned through mutual interest: Find common points of interest between your company and its user community, and work from there. Both the company and the community likely want to support user-created content, and want to increase the popularity of the products they love. Rewarding users through public recognition of their efforts is a proven method of aligning the interests of communities with your company.

Make user innovation easy: While you don't need to go as far as releasing your product's source code, plans, or secret formula, opening up some windows into your product will both encourage innovation and dissuade people from tinkering with the parts of the product you want to keep private. Toolkits are a proven way to get user input and to maintain some control over your product. However, a good toolkit takes as much time to create as any other high-quality product, so do what game companies do and plan the development of your toolkits from the beginning of the product creation process.

Endnotes

1. Hector Postigo, "Of Mods and Modders: Chasing Down the Value of Fan-Based Digital Game Modifications," *Games and Culture* 2 (2007): 300-313.

2. Steve Wozniak, "Pirates Letters Answered," *Woz.org*, http://www.woz.org/letters/pirates/10.html.

3. Eric von Hippel, *Democratizing Innovation* (MIT Press, 2005).

4. Ibid.

5. Ben Kuchera, "Sony PSP Handheld Entertainment System: Page 1," *Ars Technica* (Mar. 28, 2005).

6. Andrew Yoon, "Ridiculous PSP Piracy Numbers," *PSP Fanboy* (Mar. 9, 2008); and Aleks Krotoski, "Hacking the PlayStation Portable," *Technology Review* 108 (2005): 70.

7. Mike Musgrove, "Tapping into Tinkering: Some Makers of Electronics Benefit from Users' Modifications," *The Washington Post* (July 12, 2005).

8. R. Rosenbaum, "Secrets of the Little Blue Box," *Esquire Magazine* (1971): 116; and Ethan Mollick, "Working with the Underground," *Sloan Management Review* (Summer, 2005).

9. D. Kushner, *Masters of Doom: How Two Guys Created an Empire and Transformed Pop Culture* (Random House Trade Paperbacks, 2004).

10. Wagner James Au, "Triumph of the Mod," *Salon* (Apr. 16, 2002).

11. Julien Wera, "Online Community Management: Communication Through Gamers," *Gamasutra* (Apr. 1, 2008).

12. L. B. Jeppesen and L. Frederiksen, "Why Do Users Contribute to Firm-Hosted User Communities? The Case of Computer-Controlled Music Instruments," *Organization Science*, 17 (2006): 45-63.

13. K. R. Lakhani and R. G. Wolf, "Why Hackers Do What They Do: Understanding Motivation and Effort in Free/Open Source Software Projects," *Perspectives on Free and Open Source Software* (2005): 3-22.

14. Seth Schiesel, "In a Virtual Universe, the Politics Turn Real," *The New York Times* (June 7, 2007).

15. N. Franke and F. Piller, "Value Creation by Toolkits for User Innovation and Design: The Case of the Watch Market," *Journal of Product Innovation Management,* 21 (2004): 401-415.

16. R. Prügl and M. Schreier, "Learning from Leading-Edge Customers at The Sims: Opening Up the Innovation Process Using Toolkits," *R&D Management* 36 (2006): 237-250.

17. S. Thomke and E. von Hippel, "Customers as Innovators: A New Way to Create Value," *Harvard Business Review* 80 (2002): 74-81.

18. L. B. Jeppesen, "User Toolkits for Innovation: Consumers Support Each Other," *Journal of Product Innovation Management* 22 (2005): 347-362.

19. K. R. Lakhani and E. von Hippel, "How Open Source Software Works: 'Free' User-to-User Assistance," *Research Policy* 32 (2003): 923-943.

20. C. Baldwin, C. Hienerth, and E. von Hippel, "How User Innovations Become Commercial Products: A Theoretical Investigation and Case Study," *Research Policy* 35 (2006): 1291-1313.

CHAPTER 10

WHY GAMERS ARE BETTER THAN COMPUTERS, SCIENTISTS, AND GOVERNMENTS

In 2006, Netflix, the DVD rental company, offered a $1 million prize to anyone who could substantially improve "Cinematch," the formula used by Netflix to recommend movies to its customers. Cinematch works by comparing the way that you have rated movies to the way that other Netflix customers have rated movies. When Cinematch detects a pattern, it uses that information to recommend movies you haven't seen yet, but that people like you have rated highly. Cinematch is an important driver of revenue for Netflix, which explains why the company hoped to lure computer scientists and statisticians into improving the system's accuracy.[1] To aid these scientists, Netflix publicly released 100 million old movie ratings from its database, which researchers could use to develop and test new versions of Cinematch. In response, 20,000 teams took up the Netflix challenge, including many from top universities all over the world.

Of all the competing teams, the one formed by Jay Sandhaus and Andrew Bergmann was perhaps the most inventive. While most approaches to the Netflix challenge have involved elaborate statistical models, Sandhaus and Bergmann felt this was ultimately the wrong direction. "I deal all the time with people who try to solve human problems, like rating movies, exclusively with technology," Sandhaus explained, "but we have to treat people as people, and not as computers. We need to put the problem in human form and see what comes out." In other words, the way computers approach suggestions ("If you like *Wag the Dog,* you'll love *101 Dalmatians*") is much different from the way people do. To build a better formula, Sandhaus and Bergmann needed thousands of people to do the same thing manually that the Cinematch formula does automatically: give suggestions based on past movie ratings. And so *Video Store Clerk* was born.

Video Store Clerk is a casual game in which you play the role of (surprise!) a video store clerk. Your job is to give movie recommendations to an endless stream of virtual customers. Using the old, anonymous data shared by Netflix, *Video Store Clerk* tells you some of the movies that a customer has liked and disliked in the past. You are then asked to guess how the customer would rate a specific movie. You might not realize it, but by playing the game and helping virtual customers, you're actually helping Sandhaus and Bergmann improve Cinematch.

Video Store Clerk quickly exposes how difficult it is to predict the way people rate movies, and why computer algorithms quickly run into trouble. Some Netflix customers rate all movies either four stars or five stars, whereas some use the full range of available ratings. Some people seem to like certain actors, whereas others prefer particular film styles. As you play *Video Store Clerk,* these preference patterns begin to emerge, and you find yourself able to comprehend Netflix's customers in a way that machines simply cannot. For example, a machine might be confused by a person who hates *You've Got Mail* but likes *Better Off Dead* and *Sixteen Candles,* but a movie buff could potentially guess that this particular customer likes 1980s teen comedies, but dislikes romantic films in general. And, indeed, movie buffs have flocked to *Video Store Clerk,* racking up hours of gameplay while trying to achieve a top score.

Figure 10.1 *Video Store Clerk* makes it fun to improve the Cinematch algorithm.

Video Store Clerk is a great illustration of the way in which games can be used to harvest knowledge from thousands or even millions of people, but it is just the beginning. Games are now being used to solve problems that computers cannot easily solve, to generate novel ideas, and to make predictions about the future—which we call human computation, distributed innovation, and prediction, respectively. With their unique capability to focus the attention of millions of people, games are rapidly becoming a way for organizations to solve the hardest problems in the most innovative ways.

Human Computation

Human computation is the reverse of the usual relationship between people and machines. Whereas computers normally solve problems for people, human computation games help computers outsource difficult problems back to us. Players of *Video Store Clerk* voluntarily help Sandhaus and Bergmann improve the Cinematch formula, simply because they enjoy playing the game. In a way, *Video Store Clerk* is like Mark Twain's Tom Sawyer, convincing the neighborhood kids that whitewashing a fence is fun. The main difference between the two is that Tom Sawyer could have eventually painted the fence on his own, but human computation games can solve problems that would otherwise go unsolved by computers, or go poorly solved at best.

In fact, it turns out that there are many areas where human intelligence is still superior to computing power. For example, computers are very bad at identifying images, which has become an increasingly important problem as millions of new photos and illustrations are uploaded to the World Wide Web each year. Luis von Ahn, Assistant Professor at Carnegie Mellon University and winner of a MacArthur Foundation "genius" grant, developed *The ESP Game* to help solve this problem.

In *The ESP Game*, two anonymous players are matched online without any means of communicating with one another. Both players are shown a random image (for example, a flowering plant under a clear sky) while a clock counts down two and a half minutes. The players must then type words that describe the image, such as "plant," "flower," "pretty," or "sky." When both players have typed at least one word in common, like "sky," they both score points and a new picture is shown. At this moment, the players have helped teach the computer that this picture contains a "sky."

This goes on until the players have run out of time. In an interesting twist, sometimes pictures get recycled by the game after they have already been labeled once. When this happens, the old label (i.e., "sky") is no longer accepted by the game, so players must come up with a second or third word to describe the picture. In this way, the game forces players to give each picture a more detailed description.

The ESP Game is undeniably addictive. Many people play for over 20 hours a week, and more than 20 million labels have been harvested in just a few years—the equivalent of several million dollars of free labor. Professor von Ahn estimates that just 5,000 people playing *The ESP Game* for a month—a tiny number compared to the active populations of many gaming Web sites—could label every image on the Web. In fact, Google found *The ESP Game* to be so useful that it licensed the game for its own use, as the "Google Image Labeler."

Hacking with Human Computation

Professor von Ahn is famous for another innovation: CAPTCHA, the weirdly distorted letters that you see when registering for a free e-mail account or similar online service. CAPTCHAs are used to make sure that a real human being, and not an automated program, is signing up for a product or service. This is important in the case of free e-mail accounts, such as Gmail and Yahoo! Mail, because junk e-mail senders are always looking for disposable accounts through which they can send their spam.

But the spammers have struck back, ironically by using the same human computation technique that Professor von Ahn pioneered. Their approach involves a provocative game on the Web, in which a scantily clad virtual woman removes an article of clothing when a player correctly identifies a distorted word. That word, of course, is a CAPTCHA taken from another Web site. Thus, each word entered, and each piece of clothing removed, enables the spammer to circumvent a CAPTCHA and create another free e-mail account![2]

The ESP Game is just one of various "games with a purpose" developed by Professor von Ahn. *Peekaboom* refines the data gathered by *The ESP Game* by encouraging players to identify the parts of a picture that are associated with a given label. For example, two players of *Peekaboom* might be shown the picture of the flowering plant under a clear sky. The first player, seeing the label "sky," might correctly click the blue region above the flowing plant. The second player must then guess the correct label, solely by seeing what region of the picture was selected by the first player. If the second player guesses "sky," both players score points.

The techniques pioneered by Professor von Ahn may soon be applied to many other real-life problems. For example, the Transportation Security Administration has expressed interest in creating a game in which "bags are screened at the airport and sent over secure networks to multiple players who help determine the contents of each image. This could imply a major gain in security as an aid in the baggage screening process: Instead of a single officer looking at each bag, multiple people could see each bag, having a higher chance of finding potentially dangerous objects."[3]

Human computation can even be used to unveil some of the secrets of the universe. *Stardust@home* is an effort to identify the incredibly tiny grains of interstellar dust that were collected on a special aerogel by NASA's *Stardust* spacecraft in 2006. These grains are so rare that only 40 or so are expected to have been collected by the rocket, and identifying them might take scientists over 20 years using conventional techniques. The *Stardust@home* Web site explains: "Before a 'pattern recognition' computer program can identify the telltale signs of the impact of an interstellar dust particle…it has to 'learn' the pattern from existing examples of such impacts. Since interstellar dust has never before been captured in aerogel, no such examples exist! As a result, no computer program is able to recognize the pattern. In contrast, the human eye can recognize such impacts with just a minimal amount of training."[4]

So instead of using conventional techniques, the scientists behind *Stardust@home* have farmed out short film segments of the *Stardust* aerogel to the general public, and have encouraged participation in the identification game through a scoring system that rates accuracy and participation, as well as through other prizes and incentives. Within approximately one year, 24,000 players have searched more than 40 million film segments, and have identified a number of potential dust particles.

Examining the scoreboards of *Stardust@home* reveals an interesting phenomenon—scores are far from evenly distributed. Out of 24,000 participants, most have scored just a few dozen points, but the top 1% of players have scores that average over 100 times higher. Some of these top scorers may simply be spending every waking moment on *Stardust@home*, while others might somehow be cheating, but a significant number of the top players are doing so well because they have specific skills or knowledge that makes them uniquely talented at finding space dust. In other words, games are capable not only of harnessing volunteer labor, but of helping organizations harness the talents of uniquely skilled individuals.

Distributed Innovation and Collective Intelligence

Most businesses' ability to innovate is limited by Joy's Law—named after Bill Joy, the co-founder of Sun Microsystems. Joy's Law states: "No matter who you are, most of the smartest people work for someone else." The problem isn't simply a matter of money; even companies that are flush with cash cannot hire all the best people in a field, even if they can find them. Recent research by Professor Karim Lakhani of Harvard Business School and other scholars has shown that it is usually impossible to even know who the "best people" are, since complex technical problems are often most easily solved by specialists in seemingly unrelated fields.[5] Obviously, companies can't afford to keep a wide range of specialists on staff in hope that their knowledge may one day help solve a difficult problem. So the key to escaping Joy's Law, argues Professor Lakhani, is to take advantage of the intelligence of large groups of bright people outside the walls of a company.[6]

Distributed innovation games take a different approach to gathering information than human computation games. Whereas human computation is powered by large groups of people playing a game as frequently as possible, innovation games are designed to identify and bring together those rare individuals who can creatively solve very difficult problems. In other words, human computation games are about manpower; innovation games are about brainpower.

Foldit is an example of an innovation game—one that might soon help develop new treatments for disease by exploring the secrets of protein folding. Proteins are the molecular structures that drive most of the important functions in living beings; their shape determines how they interact with other substances. A particular shape might make a protein effective at clotting blood, and a differently configured protein might prove effective at neutralizing the HIV virus. Unfortunately, determining the ideal shape of a protein can be very difficult. Even a small protein with fewer than 100 chemical components could have a huge number of configurations—about 3^{100}, to be precise.[7] There are algorithms that can be used to determine whether one protein shape is better than another, but taking advantage of them requires computers to test billions of possible shapes for each protein, which requires massive amounts of computing power. So *Foldit* takes a different approach to the problem, capitalizing on people's spatial awareness and problem-solving skills to achieve what computers cannot.

Foldit turns protein folding into a game, in which the goal is to score the greatest number of points by identifying the optimal shape of a protein. Using a colorful graphic interface, players push and pull pieces of a protein into various shapes, trying to maximize their score by eliminating chemical incompatibilities. A team-based component of *Foldit* ensures that players will work together to solve particularly tough problems. And *Foldit*'s designers can create protein puzzles for any purpose, such as the best configuration to treat a particular cancer, and then have the players try to solve it.

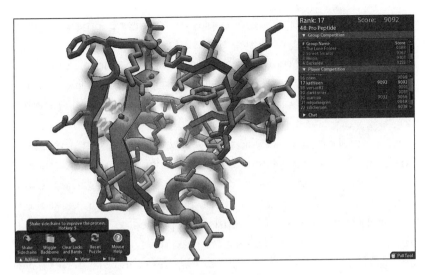

Figure 10.2 *Foldit* turns complex biochemical problems into appealing puzzles. (Courtesy of the *Foldit* team.)

One of the fascinating discoveries to come out of *Foldit* is that the best solvers of a particular problem may not be the people you'd expect. In the words of *Foldit* designer Seth Cooper, "Some of the top-scoring players are biologists, but the people who are really doing well and consistently winning don't have any biological, or even academic, background at all." Unlike a human computation game, distributed innovation depends on finding the best people to solve a particular problem, no matter who they might be. Indeed, most players of *Foldit* give up quickly and move on, but those who stay tend to be quite talented, and many become addicted to the game. And the *Foldit* team has every intention of leveraging the efforts of those talented players for the benefit of humankind. They plan to create games that will help design biofuels and vaccines, and express the hope that, someday, an innovation game player will win a Nobel prize for the work he did while "playing around."

Innovation games aren't limited to solving scientific problems, as one alternate reality game has demonstrated. For 32 days in 2007,

World Without Oil challenged its players to survive a make-believe oil shortage, which threatened the world with political, social, and economic unrest. Through blog posts, videos, diaries, and even comics, its players responded by illustrating what their lives would be like during a real oil shock, and how they were adapting to the ongoing story line. Through the shared environment of the game, players collaboratively developed ways of coping with a massive energy crisis. They grew their own food, adopted alternative methods of transportation, and reconsidered the ways they used resources. *World Without Oil* encouraged players to arrive at their own solutions to a potential crisis, as opposed to depending on a central authority for answers that may never come in an actual emergency. If not for *World Without Oil*, this group may never have gathered together, or worked collectively to answer the personal and economic questions that this game was trying to answer.

This is why Dr. Henry Jenkins, founder and Director of the MIT Comparative Media Studies Program, has argued that "ARGs [like *World Without Oil*] pretty thoroughly demonstrate the value proposition of the collective intelligence model, where diverse groups of people consciously compare notes and work through problems together. They are a fairly painless way for people to acquire skills, work together, and pool knowledge to solve problems that are more complex than any single individual can solve." Dr. Jenkins, a renowned pioneer in the field of game studies, believes that the collective intelligence-harnessing techniques used by games like *World Without Oil* will someday lead to a radical transformation of the way in which schools, universities, and corporations develop new ideas. When games are used to distribute the innovation process, it becomes possible for large, open communities to solve extremely complex problems that simply cannot be addressed by small, closed groups of handpicked experts.

Games for Prediction

In 1966, Dr. John Craven, the chief scientist of the U.S. Navy's special projects division, received a disturbing call from the Assistant Secretary of Defense that began with the sentence "I've lost an H-Bomb."[8] He informed Dr. Craven that a mid-air collision off the coast of Spain had resulted in a B-52 dropping its payload of four atomic bombs, three of which were found and one of which remained missing. Given a lack of precise information, most people in the Defense Department thought the bomb would never be found. However, Dr. Craven proved them wrong. He took a unique approach to finding the bomb—an approach that would foreshadow how games would someday be used to make predictions about the future. Instead of simply searching for the bomb, Dr. Craven gave some of the top salvage experts in the world the best information the Navy had on the location where the bomb landed, the undersea terrain of the area, and the local sea currents. Then he asked those experts to make Las Vegas–style bets on where they thought the bomb was located. By mathematically combining multiple rounds of betting, Dr. Craven came to an educated guess as to where the bomb was located. And, as a deep-diving submarine soon confirmed, his best guess was exactly where the bomb turned out to be.

Today, this method of aggregating bets to make predictions has been refined into "prediction markets," which have been used for many purposes, not just military ones. Prediction markets enable anyone to bet on the outcome of a question, such as "Will Daniel Day-Lewis win the Oscar for best actor," or "Will Jeb Bush be elected President of the United States?" The answers to these questions are traded like stocks in a stock market, and bettors are paid when their predictions come true. The price of any given "stock" (i.e., answer to a question) can then be used to figure out the probability that an event will occur. Remarkably, prediction markets have proven to be more accurate than polls in predicting election results, better than panels of experts at predicting Oscar victories, and—when used by employees of a company—extremely useful at predicting future sales of that company's products.[9]

Many economists have assumed that prediction markets work so well because they put money on the line. Their theory was that since people stood to win or lose cash based on their bets, they had great incentive to make the best possible predictions. However, new research has shown that prediction markets are much more gamelike than anything else. Whether people bet real money or artificial game points makes little difference to the accuracy of the market.[10] Furthermore, markets that have more entertaining questions tend to attract more participants, even when most of the questions are extremely serious in nature.[11] These facts suggest that prediction markets might also have the makings of terrific games.

Impact Games, the developer of the Arab-Israeli educational game *Peacemaker* (discussed in Chapter 6, "Three Skills for an Interconnected World"), has created just such a game, called *Play the News*. Each week, *Play the News* offers five minigames, each of which is based on a current news issue, ranging from political races in the United States to food crises in Africa. A short briefing introduces players to a scenario, and then asks each player to adopt the role of one of the principal figures in the scenario, such as the President of the United States or an African rebel leader. The players then decide what action they would take in that role, as well as what action they believe will actually occur in real life. One goal of *Play the News* is to educate people on current events, but another goal of the game is to harvest predictions of the future. These predictions can then be used to inform businesses, and even to educate governments and world leaders.

Another interesting approach to prediction games is the *X2 Project*. Named after the X Club, which was formed by prominent scientists who helped guide scientific development in Victorian England, the *X2 Project* is a playground for scientists. It has two components. The first component is a game-driven prediction market that encourages players to look for early signals of potentially important developments in science and technology. (The game assigns missions and points to channel predications into interesting areas.) The second component is an ARG, set in the future as predicted by the players, which allows the scientists to more deeply engage with the nature of the changes that they have predicted. *Play the News* and *X2 Project* are early examples of what is likely to be an ever-increasing number of games that help predict future events.

The possibilities could be even more interesting. Some experts have argued that prediction markets would be better at making governmental decisions than governments themselves.[12] Imagine, for example, a *SimCity*-esque game in which the player was given the financial reins of a region. The game could be set in a real location like California, could incorporate real-world constraints (that is, you can't indulge in deficit spending forever), and could dynamically import the latest real-world regional data via the Internet, such as census data and local real estate values. That way, when players begin a new game, they would be immersed in a situation that closely resembles the same situation that California's politicians are currently grappling with. But here's the catch: Once players get out of the tutorial phase, the game begins recording their decisions and transmitting them to a central database, where those decisions are aggregated into a form of a "collective vote" on what actions to take in any given situation (i.e., raise the sales tax or lower the sales tax this month). The collective choices of 100,000 game players in California might very well be better than the choices of 1,000 Californian policy experts.

Economist Robin Hanson has, in fact, argued that a government by citizens using prediction markets is preferable to that of a democracy.[13] Democracies, he believes, fail mostly because they do not do a good job of aggregating available information, something that prediction markets do very well. He even has a name for this sort of government, in which prediction markets are used to make decisions: a "Futarchy." Given that games can offer advantages of coordination, participation, and innovation over even normal prediction markets, perhaps one day the best form of government will be a "Gamearchy."

Games as the Future

We are in the early days of an extraordinary time. Games present opportunities to engage people in ways that no media before has ever made possible. Unlike books, games are interactive. Unlike television, they encourage two-way communication. Unlike movies, they demand cooperation and channel human effort. This book has touched on some of the ways in which games are transforming business by changing the way we make buying decisions, the way we learn, the way we work, and the way we innovate. But the world of games is evolving ever more rapidly, and some of the most exciting types of games—ARGs, productivity games, virtual worlds, and games for innovation—are only a few years old. The true transformation has barely begun. As new, innovative types of games are created, as the lines blur between games and reality, and as young game players increasingly assume positions of power in this world, the impact of games will become increasingly significant.

Tapping into the power of games can be like harnessing the power of an undiscovered country, full of millions of smart, eager, and motivated people who work for the sheer joy of it. Consider that in 2003, nine *billion* person-hours were spent playing *Solitaire* alone.[14] That means that while you were reading this book, in the time it took you to get to this chapter, the number of hours spent playing *Solitaire* was equivalent to the total number of person-hours required to build the Empire State Building. And in the time it took you to read this sentence, as many hours were spent playing *Solitaire* as might have been spent writing a book on games and the future of business.

Endnotes

1. Kate Greene, "The $1 Million Netflix Challenge," *Technology Review* (Oct. 6, 2006), www.technologyreview.com/read_article.aspx?id=17587&ch=biztech&pg=1x.

2. Lisa Vaas, "Striptease Used to Recruit Help in Cracking Sites," *eWeek* (Oct. 31, 2007), www.eweek.com/c/a/Security/Striptease-Used-to-Recruit-Help-in-Cracking-Sites/.

3. "TSA Mulls Video Game Development to Improve Screener Workforce," *Defense Daily* 235.21 (July 31, 2007).

4. "Stardust@home FAQ," *The Planetary Society*, accessed May 2008 www.planetary.org/programs/projects/innovative_technologies/stardustathome/facts.html.

5. K.R.Lakhani, L.B.Jeppesen, P.A.Lohse, and J.A.Panetta, "The Value of Openness in Scientific Problem Solving," Harvard Business School Working Paper No. 07—050 (2007), http://www.hbs.edu/research/pdf/07—050.pdf.

6. K.R.Lakhani and J.A. Panetta, "The Principles of Distributed Innovation" *Innovations* 2.3 (Summer 2007): 97-112.

7. D. Baker, "Proteins by Design," *The Scientist* 20.7 (2006):26.

8. S. Sontag and C. Drew, *Blind Man's Bluff: The Untold Story of American Submarine Espionage* (Harper Paperbacks, 2000).

9. J. Wolfers and E. Zitzewitz, "Prediction Markets," NBER working paper (2004).

10. E. Servan-Schreiber et al., "Prediction Markets: Does Money Matter?" *Electronic Markets* 14.3 (2004): 243-251.

11. B. Cowgill, J. Wolfers, and E. Zitzewitz, "Using Prediction Markets to Track Information Flows: Evidence from Google," working paper (2008).

12. Robert W. Hahn and Paul C. Tetlock, "Using Information Markets to Improve Public Decision Making," *Harvard Journal of Law and Public Policy* (Summer 2003) http://ssrn.com/abstract=598882.

13. R. Hanson, "Shall We Vote on Values, but Bet on Beliefs?" George Mason working paper (2003).

14. Luis von Ahn, "Human Computation," *Wired Science* (PBS, 2007), www.pbs.org/kcet/wiredscience/story/96-luis_von_ahn_human_computation.html.

GAMES INDEX

INDEX

Index

Y-Z